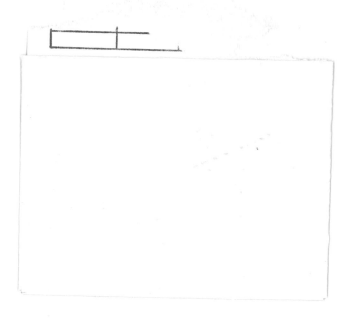

Analyzing Soviet
Strategic Arms Decisions

Other Titles of Interest

U.S. Intelligence and the Soviet Strategic Threat, Lawrence Freedman

Quantitative Approaches to Political Intelligence: The CIA Experience, Richards J. Heuer, Jr.

Soviet Involvement in the Middle East: Policy Formulations, 1966-1973, Ilana Kass

A Westview Special Study

Analyzing Soviet Strategic Arms Decisions
Karl F. Spielmann

The importance to Western policymakers of determining the significance of Soviet strategic arms decisions is matched by the difficulty of doing so. The high stakes involved and, in many cases, the inadequacy of evidence can all too easily lead to generalizations that rest more on passionate conviction than on accepted principles of scholarly inquiry. This book provides a framework for determining where we are and where we can go in analyzing Soviet strategic arms behavior.

Dr. Spielmann, urging the use of multiple-approach analyses rather than reliance on a single analytic view, presents three approaches that might be pursued in juxtaposition in examining individual Soviet strategic arms decisions. The first two basically reflect two broad schools of thought on the Soviet-U.S. strategic arms relationship; they stress, alternatively, responsiveness to the international threat and internal bureaucratic and organizational processes as shapers of strategic arms programs. The third approach represents a middle ground that heretofore has not been emphasized. These three approaches are outlined without extensive elaboration to give an initial indication of the usefulness of juxtaposing discrete sets of analytic assumptions in addressing the whys and wherefores of a particular Soviet strategic arms decision. In the concluding chapter, the author demonstrates how a multiple-approach analysis might be begun in the case of the first Soviet ICBM, and gives suggestions for undertaking further analytic tasks of this sort.

Karl Spielmann received his Ph.D. in political science from Harvard University. An analyst on the staff of the Institute for Defense Analyses, specializing in Soviet defense and foreign policy, he is coauthor (with Matthew P. Gallagher) of *Soviet Decision-Making for Defense: A Critique of U.S. Perspectives on the Arms Race.*

Analyzing Soviet
Strategic Arms Decisions
Karl F. Spielmann

Westview Press / Boulder, Colorado

355.0335

Sp4a

106968

Oct. 1978

A Westview Special Study

Published in 1978 in the United States of America by
  Westview Press, Inc.
  5500 Central Avenue
  Boulder, Colorado 80301
  Frederick A. Praeger, Publisher

Library of Congress Cataloging in Publication Data
Spielmann, Karl F.
  Analyzing Soviet strategic arms decisions.
  (A Westview special study)
  Includes bibliographical references.
  1. Russia—Military policy. 2. Russia—Armed forces—Weapons systems.
3. Munitions—Russia. I. Title.
UA770.S75   355.03'35'47   78-6007
ISBN 0-89158-162-6

Printed and bound in the United States of America

To my parents

Contents

Preface

This study was originally undertaken as a contribution to a project on the Soviet-U.S. strategic arms relationship conducted by the historian, Office of the Secretary of Defense. The overall project task was (1) to set forth a historical record of Soviet and U.S. strategic programs and policies for the period from 1945 to May 1972 (the conclusion of SALT I), and (2) to evaluate, on the basis of that record, various arms race hypotheses, particularly the action-reaction hypothesis. This study was designed to contribute to that evaluation by probing the Soviet defense decision-making environment with a particular view to identifying and analyzing the possible impact of Soviet bureaucratic factors on Soviet strategic arms decisions.

It became evident in the course of the analysis that even with a much more extensive evaluation of the Soviet decision-making environment than was feasible with the study resources, the impact of bureaucratic factors was and is likely to remain quite uncertain. That the data to support any findings would be meager was apparent from the start. What the analysis brought into sharper focus was that the evidence could in fact be taken to support a variety of interpretations, depending critically on the analytical assumptions that one brought to it in the first place.

Should this provide grounds for despair or for a kind of analytical anarchy where "anything goes" because strict standards of scholarship cannot readily be met? Should it provide an excuse to rest content with analyses that avoid explicit treatment of the Soviet decision-making setting in interpreting strategic arms issues?

This study prefers to draw different conclusions from the nature of the evidence—the principal one being that decision-making analyses do not so much create new data problems as they expose existing gaps in our understanding, and in that there is a virtue. The task at hand thus is to try to utilize that virtue for guidance in evaluating Soviet strategic arms decisions without nurturing a new dogma in the process.

Karl F. Spielmann
Arlington, Virginia

Acknowledgments

With the standard caveat that nobody but the author should be held responsible for the arguments advanced herein, several important debts deserve public acknowledgment. To the Institute for Defense Analyses, the Defense Advanced Research Projects Agency, and to the Office of the Historian, Department of Defense, special thanks are owed for making the study possible in the first place. To my long-term colleagues in IDA in the International and Social Studies Division—and to a new IDA colleague, Dr. Glenn Buchan—who provided much helpful advice, I also owe a large debt. To Dr. Alfred Goldberg (historian, Office of the Secretary of Defense) personally, and to the many participants in the strategic arms history project conducted by Dr. Goldberg, much appreciation is due for the education I received from them in the course of the project. To Dr. Matthew Gallagher, former colleague at IDA and cherished friend, I owe the debt due one who has provided a model of how to combine prudence and insight in dealing with a topic that can easily exact sacrifice of one or both of these scholarly virtues. And finally, I am particularly grateful for the secretarial assistance of Patricia Denny, who did everything possible to get this book in shape, short of illuminating the manuscript.

K.F.S.

Introduction

We just do not have an adequate explanatory model for the Soviet-American arms race.[1]

Since World War II, the strategic arms relationship between the United States and the Soviet Union has been the principal fact of life in the international arena. For the Western policymaker, new and legitimate concerns of international scope—energy, food, nuclear proliferation, terrorism—have been thrust to the fore in recent years. Yet the mutual antagonism of the two superpowers and their capability to destroy each other and the rest of the world as well make their strategic arms relationship an international security problem of enduring and overriding import.

One of the more disquieting aspects of the problem is that in many ways it is so little understood. It is readily apparent that the strategic nuclear arsenals of both the United States and the Soviet Union have, in the main, increased in quantity and quality in the postwar era. And it is quite evident that in the past decade or so the Soviets have made efforts to at least match the United States in strategic nuclear might. But the whys and wherefores of the Soviet-U.S. strategic arms relationship are still dimly comprehended. It is hardly surprising therefore that the basic question of the future course of the relationship should generate frequent and heated debate.

1

Assessing the International Action-Reaction Phenomenon

A particular question that has prompted much speculation but no firmly grounded answers is whether an action-
reaction phenomenon affects the strategic nuclear relations
of the two superpowers. For the policymaker concerned with
devising policies that best serve the security interests of the
United States, the most pertinent formulation of the
question is this: Do actions on the U.S. side of the strategic
equation, particularly in strategic nuclear weapon programs, prompt the Soviets to react with new or larger
programs of their own?

In seeking guidance for present policy deliberations or
future reference, it would seem prudent to begin with the
historical record. Only of late, however, has there been any
determined effort to put this record together—to trace, in
some detail, Soviet and U. S. strategic arms programs and
policies in the postwar era.[2] History may never judge, but
historians do. Interpreting the historical record, therefore, to
determine whether and to what extent the action-reaction
phenomenon has been operative in the Soviet-U.S. strategic
arms relationship requires specific attention to the assumptions that historians, or analysts in general, might bring to
this body of evidence.

Colin Gray has characterized two broad schools of
thought which, in viewing this historical record, would
yield quite divergent assessments of the role of the
international action-reaction phenomenon in the Soviet-
U.S. strategic arms relationship over the years. As he put it:

> For the past five years (at least), most politicians, bureaucrats
> and academics who have commented upon arms control have
> apparently adhered to the rather simpleminded proposition
> that to every arms race action, there must be a correspon-
> ding—in the sense of offsetting—reaction. Hence, the arms
> race "spiral" (a very dubious metaphor) is expensive,
> perennial, and politically futile. Rational strategic men,

playing a game in which they just block each other's shots, exist solely in the realm of strategic fiction.

A rival proposition is gradually gathering strength. The newer proposition holds that the arms race behavior of the state-actors is determined not so much by the perception of threat, as by "the games that bureaucrats play." The range of models for the elucidation of this proposition is formidable indeed. At one extreme, analysts devise an action-reaction model wherein the principal actors are the U.S. Air Force, Navy and Army—competing with a somewhat astrategic budget ceiling, and with the Soviet Union performing an essential game legitimization function. More work needs to be done on the domestic processes that result in arms race actions, but it is important that the role of the dynamic external threat be not unduly degraded.[3]

Most Western analysts who have tried to evaluate the Soviet-U.S. strategic arms relationship would be loath to concede that they have been either simple minded or unappreciative of the Soviet threat or that they are confined to such unpalatable alternatives for future evaluations. Yet, whatever the elements of overstatement in Gray's description, he seems to be basically correct in identifying rational actor interpretations and bureaucratic interpretations as the two principal modes of analysis that have gained currency in recent years. And he also seems to be essentially correct in implying that, notwithstanding attention to variants, nuances, and the like, a basic adherence to either broad school of thought is likely to produce certain assumptions about the nature and importance of the international action-reaction phenomenon that would not be encouraged by the other analytic perspective.

The Need for Multiple Approaches

A basic premise of this study is that assessments of Soviet defense decisions, in general, and evaluations of the international action-reaction phenomenon in Soviet strategic arms decisions, in particular, could well benefit from (1) decision-making case studies of individual decisions (or sets of decisions), and (2) the use of multiple analysis approaches in conducting the case studies. Gray's characterization of the ways we have tended to think about the Soviet-U.S. strategic arms relationship suggests that our understanding of both Soviet and U.S. strategic behavior could be strengthened by avoiding a steadfast commitment to any single approach. But there is particular reason to believe that the use of multiple approaches in examining specific strategic arms decisions is especially necessary in looking at the Soviet side of the strategic equation.

The General Question of Soviet Intentions

The need for multiple approaches can perhaps best be appreciated if we bear in mind that the question of the role of the international action-reaction phenomenon in Soviet strategic arms decisions is but part, albeit a most important part, of the general question of why the Soviets develop, produce, and deploy weapon systems—of particular types, in particular numbers, at particular times. As important as it may be to know that the Soviets have a particular weapon in hand, or that that weapon is in the offing, an understanding of its significance for the United States (and, in fact, any basic estimate of likely future directions of Soviet weapon efforts in general) may also call for an evaluation of Soviet intentions.

The inherent difficulty of divining the purpose (or purposes) behind weapon systems could be circumvented by evaluating those systems on a worst-case basis and devising appropriate U.S. countermeasures accordingly. Cost considerations, among others, make it unlikely, however, that the problem could be finessed in this manner even for Soviet strategic systems that appear to be of great concern to the United States from a national security standpoint—much less for Soviet systems across the board. The question of priorities, both military and civilian, constrains the effective use of worst-case planning by the United States in dealing with new or emerging Soviet capabilities.

But even when a particular Soviet weapon system cannot be treated on essentially a worst-case basis, the difficulty of evaluating the significance of that system for the United States does not have to be overwhelming. The performance characteristics of the system, which in the main seem susceptible to "hard" quantification and calculation, would be an obvious help in assessing likely Soviet motives behind the system. Without discounting the possibility of Soviet blunder, a Soviet missile, for example, that was assessed to have a certain range capability would probably not have been built by the Soviets for the purpose of striking targets beyond that range. At the same time, however, performance characteristics may yield only partial or ambiguous answers about Soviet intentions. Indeed, even assessing what capabilities these characteristics really represent may go beyond what hard quantification and calculation can tell us. For that assessment also calls for some judgment on the Soviet perception of these characteristics. This perception may or may not be unique, but in any event cannot merely be assumed to be obvious on the basis of the technical data alone.

It is because the policymaker and, in turn, the analyst are confronted at this point with the need to deal with skimpy and soft data[4] that attention to Soviet defense decision making and the use of multiple analytic approaches are commended. Pressure to come up with answers regarding the significance of Soviet weapon efforts means that assumptions will be made about Soviet intentions in any event, at times with little regard for even minimal standards of scientific inquiry.

It is a situation fraught with irony. Analysts evaluating comparatively hard data on the technical aspects of Soviet weapon systems can be expected to appreciate that the physical sciences no longer abide by the mechanistic certainties of the Newtonian universe. Heisenberg, Einstein, and others have taught them better. However, with respect to the comparatively soft data on other aspects of those Soviet weapon systems, with which the social sciences should deal and regarding which an appreciation of uncertainty and probability is even more in order, the contingent nature of our understanding can easily be honored in the breach.

What Decision-making Analyses Can and Cannot Do

Attention to Soviet defense decision making can help us keep our social science understanding of Soviet weapon efforts—and, especially, the strategic arms relationship—in proper perspective. Because of the importance that is attached to knowing what the Soviets are up to, it is tempting to oversell particular but nevertheless partial insights into Soviet behavior. But doing so can be a real disservice, since a worthwhile contribution to understanding the Soviets is more likely to be ignored than heeded if it is burdened with excessive claims.

Over the years, several different ways of looking at the Soviets have been particularly susceptible to this burden. It is one thing to acknowledge that the Soviet state is heir to certain longstanding Russian traditions and geopolitical concerns, and quite another to intimate that current Soviet behavior can somehow be comprehended as the product of some sort of Russian historical determinism. It is one thing to appreciate that the Communist ideology is likely to cause the Soviets to behave somewhat differently from the way a non-Communist Russian regime might behave, and quite another to regard the ideological pronouncements of Lenin (or any of his successors) as a master plan dictating Soviet actions. And it is one thing to pay heed to Soviet military doctrine as an indicator of peculiarly Soviet goals and practices in the military field, and quite another to treat this doctrine as an unambiguous guide to Soviet peacetime military procurements or behavior in the event of war.

Decision-making analyses can also be oversold and, as Gray has suggested, tempt one to believe that selfish organizational and bureaucratic interests hold the key to explaining U.S. or Soviet strategic arms decisions. If one steps back a bit from the recent application of decision-making analyses as described by Gray, it should be apparent that *decision making* comes close to being as value-neutral a notion as can be found in the social sciences. There is no more reason to regard decision making as the exclusive province of one particular point of view about why decisions are made than there would be to use the term *government* solely in connection with authoritarian regimes. Only to the extent that *decision making* implies that the actions one wishes to explain are *decisions* of some sort and at some level, does the term itself carry a substantial built-in bias.

In trying to explain why certain Soviet strategic arms decisions occur, we inevitably make some assumptions about Soviet decision-making practices, even if we do not explicitly treat them. If we argue, for example, that the Soviets have pushed ahead with a particular weapon system to achieve a certain hard-target kill capability against the intercontinental ballistic missile (ICBM) force of the United States, we are ipso facto arguing that the decision-making process (for that decision at any rate) was such that the consideration of the system's hard-target kill capability could emerge as a (or the) prime determinant of the Soviet decision. Since assumptions of this nature underlie any explanation of Soviet strategic arms decisions, decision-making analyses need not have a narrow compass. Indeed, to the extent that it seems to make sense to explain certain Soviet strategic arms decisions in terms of Russian historical aspirations, or Communist goals, or the requirements of Soviet military doctrine, or whatever, the various explanations of Soviet behavior that were prominent before decision making became a lively topic might now be legitimately included within its purview.

Decision-making analyses can thus contribute to our understanding of Soviet strategic arms behavior by specifically addressing the assumptions about decision-making practices that underlie the explanations we routinely offer about why Soviet strategic arms decisions occur. These assumptions may be valid, but then again they may not be. Explicit treatment of them would seem indispensable if we are to make some reasonable judgment on this score and, in turn, to gauge the utility of the explanations that rest on these assumptions. To make a contribution, however, decision-making analyses must focus on both the decision-making processes and the array of considerations that might go into these processes—such as strategic goals, organizational interests, and the like. Eventually, perhaps, these decision-making analyses may yield two rough sets of correlations: (1) between certain kinds of decision-making processes and certain kinds of strategic arms decisions, and (2) between certain kinds of decision-making processes and certain kinds of decision-making considerations.[5] In short, an extensive effort to apply decision-making analyses to Soviet strategic arms programs may, in due course, permit us to make some informed judgments as to the probability of a particular strategic arms decision having been determined by particular considerations.[6]

None of this means, however, that even a thorough knowledge of how Soviet strategic arms decisions are made would enable us to firmly explain why they are made. We are probably very far from knowing how the process really works for even a single Soviet strategic arms decision—much less what the processes might be for many of these decisions. But, it is important to remember as well that it is not only the processes that matter, but what goes into them. Insofar as such inherently soft topics as *goals, interests, preferences,* and the like are the ingredients that are processed in the making of decisions, they will limit the firmness of our conclusions. And, with respect to attaining knowledge both about how Soviet strategic arms decisions are made and about the various ingredients that the decision-making processes have to deal with, the Soviet defense setting is not forthcoming with its evidence. Accordingly, even if we constructed the most sophisticated decision-making model, incorporating all the latest pertinent social science advances, it could not spin straw into gold. It could not provide more and better evidence than the Soviet defense environment will yield.

The Nature of the Data Should Determine Decision-making Approaches

The data constraints we confront in analyzing Soviet strategic arms decisions make the use of multiple decision making approaches particularly imperative. The skimpiness and softness of the data should condition our concerns. Because the data are skimpy, we must avoid unnecessarily excluding any potentially useful evidence. It is in the nature of analytic approaches to emphasize certain kinds of evidence and to exclude (or, at the very least, slight) other kinds of evidence. In short, we should not compound the data problem.

The softness of the data means that the conclusions we draw from any single approach may often seem much firmer than they really are—both to the analyst and to the policymaker he informs. Lacking sufficient evidentiary correctives as a guide, the analyst must be particularly aware of the strengths and weaknesses of the assumptions he brings to the evidence. In setting forth a particular approach in a decision-making analysis, some explicit conceptualization of assumptions will take place—or at least it should, since without it one is not really articulating an approach at all. But even so, without being taken to task by contrary assumptions, in the course of analysis our appreciation of the tenuousness of our original assumptions can all too

easily get lost.[7] Multiple approaches offer some help both in
ensuring that certain kinds of evidence are not overlooked
(or slighted) and in aiding us in maintaining our perspective
about the firmness of the conclusions drawn from any single
approach.

There are admittedly both basic weaknesses and basic
strengths to be reckoned with in the very use of multiple
approaches to Soviet defense decision-making. The principal weakness is that unless the analyst is to present the
policymaker with a number of different answers to the same
question, some final amelioration, weighting, or the like
will have to be made. This is hardly a novel task, however,
since presumably some sort of overall judgment has to be
rendered when but a single approach is used.

Moreover, the particular answers yielded by different
approaches in a given case may not be equally persuasive.
When using multiple approaches, it is to be expected that the
utility and persuasiveness of the individual approaches
employed will vary. One must, as has been noted, be sensitive
to the differences in Soviet strategic arms decisions, in terms
of the kinds of weapons to be analyzed, the domestic context
and the international context at the time that the decisions
are taken, and so on. Depending on these circumstances, one
or more of the approaches used may prove inherently
stronger than the others. Relatedly, whatever the presumed
strengths of particular approaches to different Soviet
strategic arms decisions, the data problem will also affect
their usefulness. Multiple approaches are designed to keep
us from overlooking certain kinds of data that otherwise
might be slighted. But in each decision-making case, it
would seem likely that there would be significant differences
in the quality and quantity of data that the individual
approaches can work with. The point, however, is not to
simply write off the attempt to use multiple approaches in
the first place. In short, the task of arriving at an overall
judgment when multiple approaches are used will not be

overwhelming, but it will nevertheless probably be a bigger one than a single approach presents simply because of the additional variables involved.

Multiple approaches have a particular strength that commends their use in preference to some new combined approach that would seek to lump a variety of assumptions together within a single analytic framework. As will be discussed later, the discrete approaches that can be used to examine Soviet defense decision making each stress important factors, such as strategic calculation or bureaucratic motive, the distinctiveness of which is likely to be compromised by merely combining them. It would be difficult to prevent the new unified theory, for example, from having on the whole either a basic strategic calculation or a bureaucratic motive bias. Hence, other factors may well be taken into account, but only sufficiently so to assure skeptics that the analyst had been broad-minded.

Multiple Approaches and the Action-Reaction Phenomenon

A presumptive case can be made for the use of multiple approaches in assessing the impact of the international action-reaction phenomenon on Soviet strategic arms decision making. Evaluating whether, how, and to what extent U.S. strategic arms programs affect Soviet programs is part of the larger question of why the Soviets develop, produce, and deploy particular weapon systems, in particular numbers, at particular times. If the policymaker could count on being able to deal with Soviet programs on a worst-case basis, both now and in the future, the need to get some fix on Soviet motives and the need to understand, in particular, the impact of U.S. programs on the Soviets would be perhaps less pressing. Similarly, if the policymaker, and in turn the analyst, could rely on the performance characteristics of Soviet weapons, and especially the technical characteristics of strategic arms to tell the story about Soviet intentions, the task of assessment might basically involve arriving at the relative certainties that the physical sciences make possible.

In many instances, however, acting on a worst-case basis or relying on hard technical data may not suffice to meet the policymaker's requirements. Because there is legitimate concern about the dangers and the costs with which new Soviet weapon systems might confront us, it becomes particularly important to know, in the strategic arms field, whether, how and to what extent U.S. actions prompt Soviet reactions. And, unfortunately, to a considerable extent the answers to these questions must be based on the meager and soft data on the Soviet side with which the social sciences have to deal.

It is the importance and the nature of a determination of the international action-reaction phenomenon in Soviet strategic arms efforts, therefore, that at bottom commend the use of multiple approaches in individual decision-making cases. Since decision-making analyses using multiple approaches cannot force the Soviets to provide us with more and better data, these analyses are not going to perform miracles for the analyst or the policymaker. What they can do is to help ensure that available data are not overlooked and that our sensitivity to the assumptions we bring to the data is heightened.[8]

Insofar as the question of the significance of Soviet strategic arms programs is of pressing concern to U.S. policymakers, surely this speaks to a need that is general, real, and not insignificant. Assumptions will be made in any event—about long-term Soviet international ambitions, about specific Soviet ambitions in the case of a particular weapon system, about how the relevant Soviet decisions come about, and so on. To the extent feasible, it is incumbent on the analyst to be conscious of his assumptions and subject them to constant challenge. In fact, by making and keeping his assumptions explicit, he may be able to perform the equally important service of offering the policymaker more and better criteria to assess his findings.

Study Plan

This study only commences what is a very large task. A substantial appreciation of the strengths and weaknesses of our assumptions about how Soviet strategic arms decisions are made and what we really can know about the role of the international action-reaction phenomenon in shaping Soviet strategic arms decisions suggests the need for a series of case studies in which multiple approaches are used. Evidence should be gathered in the first place with the guidance of those approaches; the approaches should be modified and refined as the accumulated evidence suggests; a taxonomy of decisions (under the broad rubric of strategic arms decisions) should be developed on the basis of several cases, and so on.[9] With this taxonomy in hand, we might then begin to offer some informed judgments regarding the likely impact of particular Soviet motives (and in turn U.S. actions as one of those motives) in determining particular strategic arms decisions—as suggested above. We can hardly hope, however, and it is not the intention of this study to suggest, that, even with a monumental research effort using all available data, decision-making case studies of the kind that might be done on the U.S. side of the strategic equation can ever be done on the Soviet side.

The Preliminary Nature of the Study

What this study reasonably hopes to accomplish is to offer some appropriate words of caution for current efforts to interpret the Soviet-U.S. strategic arms relationship and to point the way for future efforts to examine Soviet strategic arms programs and policies in decision-making terms. It specifically seeks to call attention to the basic assumptions about the Soviet defense decision-making environment that flow from particular approaches and the general implications that those assumptions in turn hold for assessing the impact of the action-reaction phenomenon for Soviet strategic arms programs.

Part 1 of the study puts forth three approaches (labeled rational strategic actor, pluralistic, and national leadership) that are quite distinct in their decision-making assumptions and that when used together would seem to be particularly helpful in trying to explain Soviet strategic arms decisions. Part 2 evaluates certain prominent organizations, personalities, and practices in the Soviet defense decision-making environment to see whether, in fact, presently discernible Soviet realities at least basically support the use of the three approaches. Part 3 presents the broad implications that the approaches hold for current efforts to assess the role of the international action-reaction phenomenon in Soviet strategic arms decisions. Part 4 of the study points up problems and priorities for utilizing multiple approaches in future analyses. Factors that can affect our appreciation of the overall data problem in dealing with Soviet strategic arms decisions are discussed. And a multiple-approach analysis of the decision(s) on the first Soviet ICBM is presented to illustrate how such analyses might enrich our understanding of Soviet strategic arms decisions and possibly other defense efforts as well. The study concludes with suggestions for organizational procedures for conducting future analyses along multiple-approach lines.

Coverage of Approaches

The selection and treatment of approaches in Part 1 are conditioned by a concern to emphasize approaches that would seem to be particularly useful in highlighting certain features of Soviet defense, and especially strategic arms, decision making. Two of the approaches reflect the two broad schools of thought about the strategic arms race that Gray has identified. Unless Gray is way off the mark, these approaches can hardly be regarded as novel. Indeed, since it is in Graham Allison's pioneering study of the Cuban missile crisis that Gray's two schools of thought are perhaps best (or at least most prominently) conceptualized, the approaches are presented as particular readings of Allison's approaches—namely, the rational strategic actor approach as a specific formulation of Allison's rational actor model; the pluralistic approach as a specific formulation of Allison's organizational process and bureaucratic politics models.[10]

To the extent that the two approaches have any novel elements, they lie in the effort to adjust Allison's categories to better illuminate decisions that are (1) defense in nature, and (2) Soviet in nature. As they stand, Allison's models are basically drawn from U.S. decision-making experience. They are intended to apply to foreign policy as well as defense decision making. And their utility has essentially been demonstrated in what is surely an unusual decision-making situation (although perhaps selected by Allison for that very reason)—namely, the crisis precipitated by the emplacement of Soviet missiles in Cuba.

In addition to the approaches drawn from Allison's analyses, a third approach is presented: the national leadership decision-making approach. This is a new approach, at least insofar as the treatment of Soviet strategic arms decision making is concerned. It calls attention to aspects of Soviet strategic arms decision making that have not been adequately reflected in the two broad schools of thought in the particular readings of Allison's notions. The reader should be alerted that since it is a new approach, relatively more attention is given to it than to the others in the discussion to follow. The emphasis is a consequence of the requirement to demonstrate that there indeed is a place for this approach in the repertoire of interpretations of Soviet strategic arms decisions. This emphasis, however, should not be construed as an advocacy for the national leadership approach as the preferred analytical perspective. Just as with the other approaches, the national leadership approach is not designed to stand on its own. It omits or slights considerations that should be taken into account.

As stressed above, multiple approaches, in contrast to some unified approach, would seem to stand a better chance of giving particular decision-making factors due consideration. This means that, in the interest of emphasizing pertinent distinctions, the approaches used will be deprived of the subtlety that would give them at least a seeming respectability (or plausibility) when used individually.[11] What they lack in this regard, however, should be more than compensated for in their use together as a means to achieve, better than any single approach, an approximation of the diversity and complexity of Soviet strategic arms decision making.

Part 1
Three Decision-making Perspectives

1
Perspective I: Rational
Strategic Actor Decision Making

The rational strategic actor approach to analyzing decision making is a particular reading of Graham Allison's rational actor model. As Allison sees it, most analysts of foreign and defense policies over the years have used a rational actor approach even if they have not explicitly conceptualized it. He regards the approach thus as the classic model of foreign and defense policy evaluation, a model widely shared by analysts who otherwise might be quite at odds in their analytic assumptions.

Surveying a number of different studies, Allison writes:

What is striking about these examples from the literature of foreign policy and international relations are the similarities among analysts of different styles when they are called upon to produce explanations. Each assumes that what must be explained is an action, i.e., behavior that reflects purpose or intention. Each assumes that the actor is a national government. Each assumes that the action is chosen as a calculated solution to a strategic problem. For each, explanation consists of showing what goal the government was pursuing when it acted and how the action was a reasonable choice, given the nation's objective. The cluster of assumptions characterizes the Rational Actor Model.[1]

In brief, Allison's rational actor model assumes that events in the international arena are the purposive acts of nations behaving as unitary decision-making and decision-implementing entities. When a Soviet action—such as a diplomatic maneuver or a weapon deployment—is observed by the analyst, for example, the key question the analyst frames for himself is: What purpose or purposes are the Soviets pursuing in making this move? What do they reasonably hope to accomplish? Little attention, however, is given to the possibility that (1) the action was more inadvertent than purposive, (2) it was the consequence of biased or inept implementation of a decision or set of decisions, or (3) the original decision was the product of compromise, affected by values other than strategic values, by pulling and hauling within the governmental framework and the like. That the rational actor approach does not bring such considerations readily to mind does not mean the approach is of little value. What it means is that the approach might be usefully supplemented by approaches that pay deliberate attention to those considerations.

For the present, however, the task is to modify the rational actor approach to help it perform better the job it already does quite well. Rather than burden the approach with considerations that would blur its focus, it makes sense to sharpen its focus by emphasizing what seems truly pertinent to a rational actor evaluation of Soviet strategic arms decisions.

The Rational Actor as Strategic Calculator

Modifying the rational actor approach requires, first, stressing the importance of strategic calculation in the strict military sense in Soviet strategic arms decisions. Allison's approach focuses on strategic values that are rather broadly defined to include nonmilitary concerns—for example, political influence in the international arena. Such non-military factors are significant and should be taken into account, but not at the expense of military concerns—at least not in analyzing strategic arms decisions from a rational actor perspective.[2]

Allison's selection of the Cuban missile crisis as a case study in itself points up the need for focusing on strategic calculation in the strict military sense. In that case, vital national security concerns were at stake, and strategic calculation presumably figured importantly in the decision. If one were to extrapolate from that case in evaluating all Soviet strategic arms decisions, however, one could easily overstate the role of strategic calculation in general.

It cannot be justifiably assumed that, in strategic arms decisions (not to say other defense decisions) of less moment from a national security standpoint, strategic values would predominate in the calculations of the Soviets. But insofar as the term *strategic* is viewed in a broad sense to encompass both military and political values, a proper determination of the strategic "weight" of a Soviet decision is hard to make. Specifically identifying Soviet strategic values as military values can help in this regard by encouraging the analyst to view Soviet decisions according to a single common standard. Focusing on the military utility of a Soviet weapon system, its performance characteristics, and the like can facilitate the making of distinctions between those systems that the Soviets would be likely to view as particularly important in improving their strategic standing and those they would not. And on that basis, some judgment might be rendered as to the role of strategic calculation in shaping the decision. Even a system judged to be of considerable strategic weight would, of course, not automatically imply that strategic calculation determined the Soviet decision; but surely the chances seem greater than for a system of apparently marginal strategic importance.

Emphasizing Soviet Strategic Values

As with its treatment of the term *strategic*, Allison's rational actor approach also invites ambiguous use of the term *rationality*. Does the term *strategic rationality* mean that there are ubiquitous strategic values that make possible a common standard of rational behavior? Or are strategic values shaped sufficiently by certain national characteristics such that what may be irrational to an American strategist is rational in Soviet eyes (and vice versa)? Allison presents a variant of the rational actor model that would take into account different standards of strategic rationality,[3] but for the most part his rational actor analysis of the Cuban missile crisis assumes common Soviet-U.S. standards.

Just as it could be misleading to assume that Soviet strategists would think exactly like American strategists, it could be equally misleading to regard Soviet strategic rationality as unique. Undoubtedly there is some mix of the common and the peculiar to be reckoned with, which probably would differ over time and from decision to decision. What is necessary, however, is to avoid inadvertently weighting the scales either on the side of a strategic rationality common to Soviets and Americans alike or on the side of Soviet uniqueness.

As at least a first step in giving more attention to peculiarly Soviet strategic values, the rational strategic actor perspective encourages the use of Soviet doctrinal pronouncements pertinent to the decision to be explained.[4] At the same time, doctrine cannot be confidently regarded as the key that will unlock the mysteries of Soviet strategic arms decisions. The relationship between military doctrine and capabilities is by no means clear cut.[5] In some instances, professed doctrine may well reflect a shared perception on the part of Soviet military thinkers and top decision makers of the "rational" requirement for some weapon system to accomplish a certain task. In other instances, the doctrine may be mainly a rationalization to justify a decision that was prompted by other considerations, for example, the parochial interests of a particular armed service.[6] In this respect, Soviet doctrine should also properly be taken into account in a decision-making approach—such as the pluralistic perspective considered below—in which interservice rivalries are emphasized. But in any event, Soviet doctrine would seem indispensable for any effort to progress beyond evaluating Soviet strategic behavior simply in American terms.

Focusing on Decision Making

In pointing to the problems in utilizing Soviet doctrine as a means to discern Soviet strategic values, a further modification of the rational actor model is suggested. Until articulated by Allison, the rational actor approach did not call attention to decision making per se.

If one accepts Allison's evaluation of the widespread use of this model in the past, then it is understandable that there was little questioning of its utility and, in turn, of its assumptions about how decisions are made. It may have seemed important for analysts to devote their attention mainly (or even exclusively) to discerning plausible strategic motives to explain decisions, rather than asking what decision-making arrangements would make rational actor behavior possible. In any event, whatever the use of this model in the past, it has been those (like Allison) who have recently challenged the approach who have made decision making a live topic.

If the rational actor approach is to be used effectively to explain Soviet strategic decisions, the Soviet defense decision-making environment must be taken into account. Even if one were to try to focus solely on this approach to explain a Soviet strategic arms decision, attention to Soviet defense decision making would appear necessary. For example, in order to judge whether peculiarly Soviet strategic values prompted a particular decision, recourse to Soviet doctrine would seem useful. But one could be misled about what the doctrine really represented on its face. To argue that it exemplified a perception of an objective military requirement rather than an ad hoc rationalization of certain parochial interests would require an assessment of the decision-making setting to determine if the latter could have come into play.

In general, what this means is that it is important to substantiate rational actor interpretations of Soviet defense decisions with explicit attention to the decision-making environment in order to meet alternative interpretations on their own grounds. If a rational actor interpretation is to be convincing, it should (1) meet the traditional requirement of explaining a Soviet defense decision on strategic grounds, and (2) meet the additional requirement (raised by new approaches) of explaining how the Soviet defense decision-making setup would make such a decision possible.

The organizations, personalities, and practices that make up the Soviet decision-making environment will be examined in Part 2, and hence the decision-making assumptions of the rational strategic actor approach need only be briefly noted here. Two key assumptions would seem to underpin Soviet rational strategic actor behavior. The first is that Soviet strategic arms decisions are the product of centralized decision-making authority. It is possible that decisions that serve an "objective" Soviet strategic requirement could emerge from a situation in which pluralistic elements (services, designers, defense industrialists) are able to exert pressure or influence. But to concede such pressure (with all the selfish motives it connotes) generally is to seriously call into question the central premise of the rational strategic actor approach—that strategic calculation provides the dominant motive for Soviet defense decisions.

The viability of the rational strategic actor approach also

rests on an assumption that the central decision makers behave, in the main, as strategic calculators. Granting that the central decision makers could let considerations of a domestic or foreign policy nature affect their calculations, even without their being pressured by parochial interests, would also undercut the premises of the rational strategic actor approach.

On the whole, the assumption of centralized decision-making authority seems the stronger of the two. Whatever the changes in the Soviet system in the postwar era, there is little serious doubt that basic decision-making power is essentially held in the hands of, at most, a few men at the top. Consequently, the Soviet Union's totalitarianism would generally sustain the assumption of centralized decision-making authority in strategic arms decisions. The second assumption would be easily sustained if the top decision makers could be counted on to behave as if they were professional strategists on the Soviet General Staff—capable of rising above parochial service interests, deeply familiar with the military intricacies and implications of Soviet weapon systems and defense policies and predisposed to make defense decisions accordingly. But we know that, by and large, over the years the top Soviet decision makers have not been professional strategists. And, in contrast to top U.S. decision makers, they also have not had available the services of a sizable contingent of civilian defense strategists.[7] Rational actor approaches must be sensitive therefore to the problem of allowing for the "strategic education" of the top Soviet decision makers by military professionals without opening the door to the impact of pluralistic pressures from them.

It is only possible to note here that one of the most difficult theoretical problems in applying decision-making analyses is distinguishing between "pressure" and "advice." Advice from military professionals would seem to be indispensable if Soviet leaders are to be adequately apprised of the

significance of a given Soviet strategic arms program and
hence make a rational strategic decision on that program. In
that regard, the professionals may be said to influence the
decision by dint of their advice, but the decision cannot,
strictly speaking, be attributed to their pressure. Such access
would, however, seem to facilitate the possible application
of pressure, if the professionals so choose—and if they can
get away with it. Since it is conceivable that they could exert
pressure and still not reflect parochial interests that might
skew the decision, even pressure in this instance would not
necessarily be contrary to the premises of the rational
strategic actor approach. These considerations represent
areas where further refinements of this approach would seem
useful, but they cannot be fully explored within the study's
purview.

Overall Features of the Approach

Transforming Allison's rational actor approach into a
rational strategic actor perspective imposes new burdens on
the analyst. It calls for focusing on strategic calculation in
the strict military sense of the term. In evaluating strategic
arms programs, this means emphasizing the specific military utility of the strategic weapon in question, in light of its
performance characteristics, both strengths and weaknesses.
It requires specific attention to what may be peculiarly
Soviet in the strategic rationality underlying Soviet defense
decisions. And it imposes the burden of explaining how
rational strategic actor decisions are made in the Soviet
decision-making environment.

If it could be demonstrated that the rational strategic actor
approach had nothing substantial to offer an analyst,
obviously none of these burdens would be worth taking on.

But the approach does have an important contribution to make, whatever its problems and shortcomings. Without it (or without something like it), it would be all too easy to portray the Soviet Union in defense terms as a state in which strategic concerns counted for little.

2
Perspective II: Pluralistic Decision Making

In a book on comparative political development published in the late 1960s, Barrington Moore made the intriguing observation that most such studies tended to overstate the role of intellectuals in influencing the course of history simply because the authors of those studies were themselves intellectuals.[1] So too, strategic analysts may be predisposed to assume that decisions of some strategic significance would be made by top decision makers mainly on strategic grounds. In this respect, Allison's rational actor model may be an overstatement but probably not a caricature, of a widely held point of view. In any event, in presenting this model Allison has sought to demonstrate that there is room for explanations of defense and foreign policy decisions constructed on quite different premises.

Developments in Strategic Analysis and Sovietology

The search for alternative explanations of foreign and defense policy decisions has not been without its element of irony, especially where strategic analysis in general and sovietology intersect. On the one hand, the totalitarian model, which has been the most widely accepted model of

Soviet politics over the years, was designed to point up the
peculiar features of the Soviet form of rule as distinct from
Western democratic political systems. Yet, as noted earlier,
because of its stress on the monopoly of decision-making
power in the hands of one or at most a few leaders, the
totalitarian model appears generally supportive of the
notion of the Soviet Union behaving as a rational actor in
making foreign and defense policy decisions. But by the
same token, the distinctive features that the totalitarian
model is supposed to highlight are submerged if it is
assumed that, as a rational actor, the Soviet Union would act
as a nontotalitarian state (for example, the United States)
would act.

On the other hand, in part because the Soviet Union at
times has acted in ways that appear to defy explanation by
U.S. standards of rationality, the rational actor model has
come to be regarded by Allison (and others) as particularly
inadequate to explain Soviet behavior. As a corrective,
efforts have been made to find an explanation for "aberrant"
Soviet defense and foreign policy actions in the impact of
interest groups on Soviet decisions, the effect of the standard operating procedures of Soviet organizations on the
implementation of those decisions, and the like. The irony
is that, no less than the treatment of rational actor behavior
on the international stage, the conceptual tools employed
here clearly have their origins in the workshops of Western
pluralistic democracies. As such, those tools are not easily
used to explain why the Soviet Union has seemed to act
peculiarly on occasion without threatening to distort beyond recognition that which, above all, makes the Soviet
Union peculiar—namely, its basic totalitarian attributes.

The danger of distortion is probably less apparent now
than it perhaps should be. The totalitarian attributes of the
Soviet system as a whole have themselves become blurred.
No serious student of the Soviet political system has gone so
far as to deny that the Soviet Union is a one-party state and

that it has a planned and not a market economy. But the exact nature, extent, and effectiveness of central direction of the lives of Soviet citizens have increasingly become issues for debate among sovietologists.

The capability of the totalitarian model to accommodate elements of heterogeneity and change that have been discerned in the Soviet political system, especially since Stalin's day, has been challenged on several fronts. Studies have provided examples of individuals other than the top Soviet political leadership apparently having some impact on decisions that are made.[2] Examples have also been given of individuals apparently frustrating or impeding the implementation of top-level decisions.[3] And yet other studies have shown that there are grounds for assuming that individuals in a variety of occupations do achieve some collective identity and have an implicit interest at least in trying to get the regime to pursue policies that are especially favorable to them.[4] In general, these studies demonstrate that the classic totalitarian model of Soviet politics does leave something to be desired. Moreover, the most venturesome of them—in terms of specifically using pluralistic decision-making concepts—have convincingly argued that certain Soviet decisions, at least in the domestic sphere, can be explained in pluralistic terms.[5]

The new developments in sovietology reflected here suggest that efforts to explain Soviet strategic arms decisions from a pluralistic decision-making standpoint should not simply be written off—as there would have been a strong temptation to do if such efforts had been made while Stalin was still in charge.[6] By the same token, it is critically important for analysts to remember where the burden of proof really lies. The totalitarian image of Soviet politics has been tarnished, not shattered.[7] Accordingly, in using a pluralistic approach to explain Soviet strategic arms decisions, one must take heed of at least certain gross differences that continue to obtain between Soviet society and

the Western democracies in which these pluralistic notions
are rooted. And it is equally necessary to be attentive to at
least certain gross differences between the Soviet defense
decision-making environment and the Soviet civilian setting in which this approach has thus far been most successfully applied.

Applying Allison's Pluralistic Decision-making Models to Soviet Strategic Arms Decisions

Perspective II utilizes as its central analytic construct the
concept of interest groups. In the strictest sense of the word
interest groups in Western societies are "associations"
that are formed in the private sphere to exert pressure
on public policy. But Western scholars who have most
effectively applied interest-group analysis to Soviet politics
have basically used the term in a broader sense to apply to
groups within government with particular interests to
advance. (And *government* in the Soviet Union, it is well to
remember, has a very wide compass indeed.) Perspective II
employs the term *interest group* in the latter sense in order to
identify and analyze the various components of the Soviet
defense bureaucracy whose interests may affect the development, production, and deployment of strategic weapon systems.[8]

In identifying Perspective II as a pluralistic decision-
making approach, it is recognized that the rubric is a broad
one. Allison, for example, presents two alternatives to his
rational actor model in explaining the Cuban missile crisis,
both of which qualify as pluralistic decision-making
models. Briefly put, one model, the organizational process
paradigm, views the actors in international politics not as
monolithic nations or governments, but as "constellations
of loosely allied organizations on top of which government
leaders sit."[9] Events in the international arena are treated,
accordingly, not as purposive acts of, say, the United States

or the Soviet Union, but as outputs of various U.S. or Soviet governmental organizations, constraining the choices that the top decision makers can make, shaping the decisions that are made by dint of their role in implementing them, and so on.

The other model, the governmental (or bureaucratic) politics model, also is pluralistic in that it views actions in the international arena as the result of bargaining among many players in a government—"players who focus not on a single strategic issue but on many diverse intra-national problems as well; players who act in terms of no consistent set of strategic objectives but rather according to various conceptions of national, organizational, and personal goals; players who make government decisions not by a single, rational choice but by the pulling and hauling that is politics."[10]

The essential difference between Allison's two pluralistic models appears to be the following. The organizational process model emphasizes the overall interests of particular governmental organizations and especially the significance of the standard operating procedures of those organizations in shaping the implementation of decisions. The governmental politics model stresses the importance of individuals who head up the governmental organizations and recognizes that the impact of their organizations on decisions will depend heavily on the personal bargaining skills of those individuals, their personal ties to other powerful individuals, their personal interests, and so on.

Using the broad definition of interest groups alone, as its basic analytic construct, Perspective II, however, combines the key elements of Allison's two pluralistic decision-making models. Choosing between the two would probably tend to distort the nature and extent of the pluralistic elements in the Soviet defense decision-making setting. Without taking into account the insights of the organizational process model, the organizational interests that

underlie top-level bargaining and that could exert constituent pressure on the bargainers would not be adequately
brought out.[11] Ignoring the elements of the bureaucratic politics model would mean undercutting the significance of the personality factor in particular and of top-
level bargaining in general in translating organizational
interests into an impact on policy.

Choosing between Allison's models might make more
sense if either could be exploited as fully as it might be in
analyzing decision making in a Western setting. However,
the use of these models is likely to be circumscribed in the
Soviet defense environment. For example, the organizational process model (the one pluralistic model that Allison
attempts to apply with some rigor to the Soviet side in his
Cuban missile crisis case study[12]) certainly makes a
worthwhile point in stressing the distinction between
decision making and decision implementation. But Soviet
secrecy makes it hard to determine whether what is observed
by Western analysts with respect to a strategic arms program
is the product of (1) an original high-level decision carried
out to the letter, (2) a subsequent decision that has altered the
original, or (3) the way in which appropriate organizations
have implemented the decision or decisions.

Essential Pluralistic Decision-making Elements

Allison's Cuban missile crisis study is the most visible
example of a temptation to which one can easily succumb in
applying pluralistic analyses to Soviet strategic arms
decisions. In treating the Soviet side of the strategic equation
in the Cuban missile crisis (according to his organizational
process model), he focuses principally on identifying service
interests, examining the significance of interservice rivalries,
and the like. But there are other pluralistic elements to be
taken into account, for example, branches within a service
that might precipitate intra-service rivalries, weapons

designers and their interests and rivalries that might affect weapons decisions,[13] and importantly, the ministers of the defense industrial ministries.[14] These personnel and organizational elements, charged as they are with producing Soviet weapons, warrant more than perfunctory treatment in attempting pluralistic analyses of Soviet strategic arms decision making.[15]

Finally, as with the discussion of the rational strategic actor approach, certain pertinent refinements that might be made on the present approach bear mention. Apparently nonrational (or irrational) decisions do not necessarily equate with pluralistic impact. First of all, as noted earlier, we should take into account the fact that what may seem aberrant from a U.S. perspective may be simply the result of peculiarly Soviet strategic values informing the deliberations of top Soviet decision makers—acting without being pressured by parochial interests. In addition (as will be discussed in chapter 3), Soviet leaders could depart from a rational strategic course of action (by Soviet or U.S. standards) because of other military or civilian preferences they might have—again without succumbing to constituent pressure.

On the other side of the coin, rational strategic behavior in a strategic arms decision could, on occasion, result from the exertion of pluralistic pressure. Competing pluralistic pressures with respect to some weapon system could bring about an equilibrium in which the excesses of the principal protagonists were curbed, compelling them to settle for, say the kind and level of deployment of the weapon system that would be the same as a Soviet rational strategic actor decision would produce. Pluralistic elements could also contribute to a rational strategic decision by exerting influence through the information or advice they provide. As with professional strategists on the Soviet General Staff (or other personnel in the upper reaches of the Ministry of Defense in general), who can be said to influence strategic

arms decisions by dint of the "education" they provide the
top political decision makers, so too service, designer, or
defense-industrial proponents and opponents of a strategic
arms program can provide this service. Simply by arguing
for or against the program in question they may alert the
leaders to important ramifications of the system (for
example, technical strengths and weaknesses and potential
uses) that ultimately contribute to a strategically rational
decision on the program that otherwise might not have been
made. This is not, strictly speaking, the same as exerting
pluralistic pressure, which should imply some element of
compulsion.

Distinctions in these matters can, of course, become very
fine-grained. And any future refinements on the pluralistic
approach should ultimately take them into account. For
present purposes, however, these refinements cannot be
given proper attention. Just as it seems prudent, for heuristic
purposes, to identify rational strategic arms decisions (that
is, by U.S. and/or Soviet standards) essentially with rational
strategic actor decision making, it is prudent to identify
pluralistic decision making as a type of decision making that
basically yields decisions that depart from what strict
strategic calculation would indicate.

3
Perspective III: National Leadership Decision Making

Confronted with a choice, analysts inclined to either the rational strategic actor or pluralistic interpretation of Soviet decision making might end up burlesquing the Soviet political system in defending their point of view against the other. Those of the pluralistic persuasion could do so by arguing as if the Soviet leadership did not possess a basic monopoly of power and strategic concerns counted for little. Those of the rational strategic actor school could do so by accepting uncritically a simplistic image of Soviet totalitarianism that denies the relevance, if not the very existence, of heterogeneous elements in the Soviet decision-making setting.

The Need for a Third Decision-making Perspective

Combining the two approaches or using them in tandem still would not give appropriate attention to other elements in the Soviet decision-making environment that could have an impact on Soviet strategic arms decisions. Indeed, because both approaches largely exclude those elements and because they are basically at odds with each other, determined efforts to combine them could yield only a jerry-built analytic framework lacking logic and cohesion.

Without an additional point (or points) of view on Soviet defense decision making, one would be basically encouraged to believe that Soviet strategic arms decisions would be shaped by considerations other than the strategic calculations of the top leadership only if other personalities and organizations could exert sufficient pressure to affect those decisions. What is missing is a sensitivity to the multiple concerns that can reasonably be attributed to the national leadership—not only in the Soviet Union but in other states as well.

Is it necessary for a spokesman for the wheat farmers in the Midwest, for example, to exert pressure on behalf of that group before the president takes their interests into account in a decision on grain sales to the Soviet Union? Is it necessary for General Secretary Brezhnev to be pressured by Andropov on behalf of the Soviet secret police (KGB) to hedge a Soviet agreement to greater human contacts between East and West because of the additional policing problems those contacts might pose in Eastern Europe and the Soviet Union? To the extent that such spokesmen do come forth, the special interests of their particular group would be more forcefully brought to the attention of the national leaders and have a greater chance of having an impact on the decisions. But it would be taking an exceedingly narrow view of the range of concerns that a national leader might confront in making a decision to suppose that he must be actively pressured or otherwise share power (for example, by relying on the "advice" of particular groups) in order for such interests to be taken into account.

Viewed in this light, the notion of national leadership decision making that is presented in this study is hardly novel—or indeed confined to the strategic realm. An American president or a Soviet general secretary cannot be counted on simply to exclude all but strategic considerations when faced with the need to decide on a strategic arms program—considerations that might be proximate to the strategic concern (for example, its implications for a particular armed service) or more tangential (its implications for the economy of a particular region of the country).

The necessity of giving specific attention to what all might agree is common sense is simply that, in this situation as in others, common sense can easily be honored in the breach. It is not the point here, however, to argue whether this view of national leadership has been at least implicitly taken into account in earlier studies (as some might well contend, for example, in analyses of Soviet foreign policy that pay heed to the personal concerns and power struggles of Soviet leaders in influencing Soviet foreign policy moves).[1] Nor is it our point to argue that the need to give this idea specific and rigorous analytical attention has not been acknowledged heretofore.[2] Rather, the point to be made is that deliberately focusing on the notion of national leadership decision making can aid in explaining at least certain Soviet strategic arms decisions and, from a theoretical point of view, can play an important and novel role by helping to bridge the gap between the decision-making assumptions underlying rational strategic actor and pluralistic interpretations of Soviet strategic arms decisions.

Refining the Image of Soviet Totalitarianism

The explanatory utility of the national leadership decision-making perspective can, of course, only be established in a series of case studies of particular Soviet strategic arms programs. For the present, therefore, it is pertinent to describe the general relationship of this perspective to Perspectives I and II.

Mid-range Decision-making Possibilities

In broad terms, the national leadership decision-making approach provides a middle ground between Perspectives I and II by paying heed both to the basic monopoly of power in the possession of the Soviet leaders and to the heterogeneous elements in the Soviet environment that the leaders might be expected to take into account in framing decisions and getting them implemented. What this approach basically seeks to do is to focus on Soviet leaders who are not just strategic calculators and not just individuals who might succumb to constituent pressures, but who are leaders with considerable power who have a country to run as well as defense policies to pursue and who, therefore, may have particular concerns with regard to economic, political, and other matters (of both domestic and international scope) that could influence their judgments on defense decisions. In focusing on the leaders in this capacity, the point is to indicate that one can postulate some workable relationships between centralized decision-making power and institutional pluralism in the Soviet defense decision-making environment.

National Leadership Decision Making: A Hypothetical Case

An initial postulation of such workable relationships might be made by looking at a Soviet leadership situation—a power arrangement—that would on its face appear most supportive of the assumptions that underlie the rational strategic actor perspective. Just as it may be presumed that the more the Soviet political scene bears witness to a diffusion of power at the top, the more notions of pluralistic strategic arms decision making would be supported, so too the more centralized power is in evidence the more a rational strategic actor interpretation should gain credibility. But even if one posits the utmost centralization of power, it can be shown that the basic assumptions of rational strategic actor decision making are still not automatically supported.

A strict definition of national leadership decision making—assuming this same centralization of power— would require, in the case of a decision on a particular strategic weapon system, that the decision be made by one man who had established himself clearly as *the* leader, with other Politburo members definitely subordinate to him. He would be thus in a position to act as the quintessential rational strategic actor and would have the power to make the decision solely on the basis of a strategic calculation of the weapon system's significance for the Soviet Union. However, he could also take other considerations into account while making the decision. Perhaps his decision would be affected by his personal preference for the service that would deploy it—a preference based, say, on his earlier career affiliation (for example, as a military commissar) with that service.[3] Hence he may be inclined to decide for greater production and deployment of the weapon system in question than a "rational" strategic calculus on his part would warrant. His decision could also be shaped by other preferences he might have as a national leader. For example, he may well take into account what the implications of a large production run would be for his personally desired agricultural programs, insofar as the weapon system could conflict to some extent with production of agricultural equipment. In short, depending on his preferences, his decision could be for a weapon effort that was either greater or smaller than strict strategic calculation would suggest.

Although this decision-making scenario is greatly over-simplified, it helps to bring out two basic points. First, contrary to the rational strategic actor approach, a monopoly of decision-making power cannot be automatically translated into decisions calculated solely (or even predominantly) on strategic grounds. Second, contrary to a pluralistic decision-making approach, decisions that serve the interests of some personalities or groups (other than the interests that strict strategic calculation might serve) do not automatically signify that power has been shared in some significant way.[4]

Besides embodying the assumptions that analysts bring to

a problem, approaches should suggest specific questions to be asked. Examples of the kinds of questions that the above reading of the national leadership decision-making perspective suggests are these: What personal preferences with respect to particular strategic weapon systems might the national leader have as a result of his earlier career affiliations? What are the ongoing domestic economic programs that he might have a personal interest in that could potentially affect his judgments on the weapon systems? What might be his particular political or ideological concerns in the international arena that could shape his weapon judgments?

To be sure, questions like the above have not been neglected in studies of the Soviet scene. There have been studies of the career connections between top Soviet leaders and military personalities, such as Khrushchev's ties to the so-called Stalingrad group of Soviet military leaders in World War II.[5] And, on a broader basis, there clearly has been no lack of Western efforts to probe the psyches of Soviet leaders (particularly Stalin[6]) to discern their personal preferences. Similarly, as indicated by the attention that has been paid to Khrushchev's personal concern with Soviet agricultural programs,[7] the particular economic, social, or political preferences of Soviet leaders have also been brought to light. However, such considerations have thus far not been treated in decision-making terms as composing *together* a discrete set of variables that might be profitably used to examine Soviet strategic arms behavior.

It might be noted that the economic interests cited above could of course be taken into account in a pluralistic approach to Soviet strategic arms decision making—not in terms of their reflection in the personal preferences of an "omnipotent" leader, but as the interests that a particular civilian interest group would try to bring to bear on strategic arms decisions. Although it was not done earlier in laying out the pluralistic approach, one could adhere to the assumptions of pluralistic decision-making notions and at the same time widen the perspective to include civilian as well as military interest groups in evaluating a Soviet strategic arms decision.

The same cannot be said for a rational strategic actor approach, however. It seems impossible to argue that a Soviet strategic arms decision is made on the basis of strategic calculation and at the same time allow for the possible impact of civilian considerations. Implicit in the very assumptions of the rational strategic actor approach, therefore, is the contention that Soviet defense decision making and civilian considerations are rigidly separated.

The Approaches as Ideal Types

Before proceeding to the examination in Part 2 of the extent to which discernible Soviet decision-making "realities" in fact seem to support the assumptions underlying Perspectives I-III, a caveat should be entered. The approaches presented and the decision-making notions they contain are in the most basic sense of the word *"ideal types."* The latter have long been recognized as important social science tools and their utility today is not less than when the concept of ideal types was first articulated by Max Weber—at a time when the pertinent strategic relationships involved Imperial Germany, Tsarist Russia, and the like. Ideal types (as well as their more elaborate conceptual cousins, "models") lose their value only when we forget what they are—abstractions from (and hence necessarily exaggerations of) reality—and that we routinely use them. When we forget, we can easily be encouraged to believe that what is an abstraction is in fact an objective and full description of the way things really are—whether with respect to how and why strategic arms decisions are made or with respect to some other social science topic.

The approaches in this study, hence, at best focus on only

part of the "truth," if they do that (since extensive testing of them remains to be done). They are not intended to stand on their own and for that very reason have been left in cruder form than otherwise might be advisable. The national leadership approach is clearly as deficient in offering a description of how and why Soviet strategic arms decisions occur as the other approaches. But placing it in tandem with the other approaches reminds us that each of the approaches leaves out important decision-making considerations. Fleshing out any one of these approaches with nuances, shadings, and the like, while excluding the others, would not accomplish the same thing. Indeed, it would probably encourage us to believe that we know a lot more about the whys and wherefores of Soviet strategic arms decisions than we really do.

The ideal nature of the national leadership approach as presented above should be particularly stressed. Even Stalin did not conform to the image of the omnipotent national leader, much less an omniscient one. As with the other approaches, therefore, this approach only hints at a refinement that deserves to be explored in some detail— namely, that the national leader's personal preferences would be colored not only by his personal knowledge of some topic, but also by the information (advice) he received from others. This would seem to leave some opening for at least the exertion of influence upon him. Just as a Soviet leader behaving as a rational strategic actor could be influenced by the advice he receives from, say, professional strategists on the General Staff, so too a Soviet national leader could be influenced (without being necessarily pressured) by those who keep him informed about non-strategic matters that concern him.

In addition to excluding this refinement, the approach also emphasizes an omnipotent leader to point up the fact that even if one posits a leadership situation that makes the decision maker least susceptible to pluralistic pressure, rational strategic actor decision-making notions still do not exhaust the decision-making possibilities that remain. And if that is so, then it seems highly plausible that in a more realistic Soviet leadership situation, in which less omnipotence is in evidence, national leadership decision-making possibilities would be even greater—albeit with the chances of pluralistic decision making also being enhanced.

Part 2
The Soviet Defense
Decision-making Environment

Introduction to Part 2

The utility of each of the approaches presented in Part 1 has been presumed to rest on certain broad decision-making realities that can be found in the Soviet Union. It is appropriate next to take a more deliberate look at the Soviet decision-making environment to see whether this presumption seems sufficiently justified to sustain the approaches as at least working hypotheses. In the discussion that follows, the assumptions of the national leadership approach will be the focus of attention, not because of any preference for that approach, but because, of the three approaches, it can be most usefully juxtaposed to the decision-making assumptions of the other two. Consistent with the preliminary nature of the study, the discussion does not purport to offer a comprehensive picture of the current Soviet defense decision making setting, much less a detailed account of the various changes in this setting in the postwar era.

4
The Broader Context of Soviet
Strategic Arms Decision Making

If the national leadership decision-making perspective had to rely on the assumption of an omnipotent leader in the Soviet setting, it would hardly represent much of an advance over Perspectives I and II in doing justice to Soviet political realities. National leadership decision-making considerations can, however, be taken into account in a leadership situation in which there is a sharing of power by a few men at the top, even though one individual is preeminent or, in some cases, even quite dominant. Roughly speaking, this covers the current leadership situation in the Soviet Union. It also applies, if one allows for a shifting emphasis between the one individual and the other few men, to the leadership situation during the Khrushchev period.

The Supreme Defense Council

The key question to be addressed is whether the current Soviet leadership situation is supportive of the notion inherent in the rational strategic actor approach of a rigid separation of defense decision making from the broader Soviet political and economic context. A primary consideration that would seem to lend support to the notion of rigid separation is that the Soviets have apparently adopted certain institutional mechanisms to narrow the circle of top leaders who routinely concern themselves with defense decisions. Perhaps the major mechanism in this regard, in operation today, is what Raymond Garthoff has referred to as the Supreme (or Higher) Defense Council.[1]

The name and composition of this body suggest that it is the principal arena for deliberations on strategic weapon system programs, defense policies, and the like prior to (or possibly in some cases in lieu of) formal Politburo-level decision making on these matters. Presumably intended to limit the scope and intensity of bargaining over defense programs and policies at the top political level, the council has at present at least three Politburo members as its regular members (General Secretary Brezhnev, chairman of the council; Premier Kosygin; and Defense Minister Ustinov[2]) and perhaps as many as five.

If the membership of this body comprised individuals whose sole or even main concern was defense matters, it would go a long way toward supporting the notion that the Soviets can (and do) successfully separate civilian considerations from their strategic arms decisions and, in so doing, strongly underpin the rational strategic actor approach. However, with the exception of Ustinov, the other Soviet leaders on the council have more than strategic concerns to engage their attention, whatever priority they attach to strategic arms matters in discharging their responsibilities as council members.[3] It would thus seem appropriate to hedge any assumption that the strategic arms decisions taken in the council would be made solely on the basis of an agreed strategic calculation. In some cases, to be sure, the strategic significance of a particular decision (for example, the go-ahead for a weapon system) might well be such as to override any other considerations. But it cannot be flatly maintained that, say, Kosygin, with his oft-touted consumer goods concern, would never let his input into defense decisions be affected by this concern. And it cannot be merely assumed that the other council members are schizoid policymakers either.

In addition, ruling out the intrusion of civilian consider-ations would seem to require decisions taken in the council to be routinely and passively accepted by the rest of the Politburo members as faits accomplis when those decisions reach the Politburo. There is room for doubt on this score. Indeed, decisions that appear to have the greatest strategic significance may, paradoxically, be most likely to attract the attention of Politburo members who have civilian axes to grind—precisely because decisions of this sort may well carry a considerable claim on scarce resources.[4]

None of the foregoing is intended to suggest that the Soviet Union over the years has not placed a high priority on defense, to the possible detriment of the civilian economy. Widespread acceptance of the defense sector's priority status in the top Soviet leadership circles means only that civilian concerns have probably had a noticeable impact on fewer defense (and especially strategic arms) decisions and a milder impact on those decisions they did affect. It does not mean, however, that the relevance of civilian concerns can be or should be disregarded in attempting to explain Soviet strategic arms decisions.[5]

Central Planning

That Soviet defense decisions are not made in a vacuum is reinforced by the very characteristic of the Soviet economy that has facilitated the maintenance of priority treatment for defense programs over the years—namely, central planning. Given the sizable resource claim that the defense sector places on the economy as a whole, it would be incredible if the Soviets did not make some effort to coordinate defense program planning with the overall economic plan—at least on an annual and five year basis.[6]

As the Soviets keep discovering in regard to agricultural production, however, all the relevant economic inputs and outputs cannot be precisely predicted and incorporated in these plans (especially the five-year plans). Just as weather can alter agricultural plans, so too presumably a momentous event in the international arena, an unexpected U.S. deployment decision, or a technological breakthrough by the Soviets themselves could disrupt any five-year defense plan calculations.[7] Nevertheless, if the effort to provide a five-year plan for the economy as a whole is not to be negated, at least some rough prediction must be made of the size and nature of the resource demands the defense sector will place on the economy within the planning period.

The probable existence of Soviet efforts to coordinate defense planning with the overall economic plan is also supported on institutional grounds. A recent study identifies a first deputy chairman of the State Planning Committee (Gosplan) as a former defense industries manager, which suggests that a special office within Gosplan may be charged with integrating defense planning into the central economic plan.[8]

It would be tempting to construe these indicators of midrange central planning for defense programs as supportive of the notion that the Soviet leadership is better able than it would otherwise be to make Soviet strategic arms decisions as a rational strategic actor. To the extent that the plan constrains the possibilities for interest groups within the defense sector to push programs that have not been planned for, the case for the Soviet Union behaving as a rational strategic actor is probably strengthened. Yet at the same time, the existence of Soviet five-year defense planning means basically not that the possibility of interest-group activity is largely excluded, but that it would be most likely to occur at particular times in the planning cycle—most particularly in the months immediately prior to the formal acceptance of the next five-year plan, when priorities and prospective programs would be under heavy consideration.

From the standpoint of the national leadership perspective, the (or at least a) key rationale for having a five-year defense plan argues against the premises of the rational strategic actor approach. If defense planning is a necessary part of planning for the economy as a whole, it can hardly be contended that there is a rigid separation of defense decision making from civilian economic concerns. As with the pluralistic approach, however, the impingement of civilian considerations on strategic arms programs—with Soviet leaders acting as national leaders—would appear most likely at particular intervals.

Relationships of the Three Approaches

Viewed with the assumptions of the national leadership decision-making perspective in mind, some of the key institutions and practices that can be discerned in the Soviet defense decision-making setup are misperceived if they are seen simply as creating or sustaining a rigid separation between civilian considerations and defense decisions. To be sure, the rational strategic actor approach is probably nearer the mark than the pluralistic approach in reflecting the basic realities of these institutions and practices.

The notion of national leadership decision making, however, makes allowance for aspects of these Soviet institutions and practices that the rational strategic actor approach tends to discount. The national leadership decision-making perspective thus parts company with the rational strategic actor approach by taking into account the heterogeneous elements in the Soviet decision-making setting. At the same time, it also maintains some distance from the premises of pluralistic approaches in that it does not equate the impact of various heterogeneous elements with pluralistic pressure. For example, Kosygin could bring

his concern for Soviet consumer goods industries to his
deliberation of a particular defense decision without having
been subjected to pressure, say, from N.N. Tarasov of the
Ministry of Light Industry—or any other individual or
organization closely identified with consumer goods interests. Similarly, to confine the impact of heterogeneous
elements to the defense sector itself, Ustinov may have a
personal bias toward a particular service or defense industry
or designer that could color his consideration of the strategic
worth of a given weapon system proposal—again, a
situation in which particular interests might be served
without their having, in some way, actually exerted pressure
in the making of the decision.

Nevertheless, it must be conceded that, in contrast to the
assumption of the existence of an omnipotent leader, such as
was made in the strict definition of national leadership
decision making, the leadership situation exemplified in the
above examples is clearly less at odds with the assumptions
of the pluralistic decision-making approach.[9] As discussed
earlier, the national leadership decision-making approach is
intended to flesh out some of the decision-making possibilities that lie between those typified in rational strategic actor
and pluralistic approaches. Viewed in this light, a strict
definition of national leadership decision making, assuming an omnipotent leader, probably comes closest to sharing
the assumptions that make the strongest case for rational
strategic actor decision making—although even here, as we
have seen, there are key differences between these approaches. The corollary, of course, is that the farther one goes
from the assumption of an omnipotent leader, the closer one
comes to the pluralistic end of the decision-making
spectrum.

5
The Dual Role of Pluralistic Elements

The discussion in chapter 4 indicates that the national leadership decision-making approach has a contribution to make in offering explanations of Soviet defense decisions that a rational strategic actor approach would not make. But, it may well be asked, where does the relevance of the national leadership approach leave off in this leadership situation and the relevance of pluralistic approaches begin? Or, to put it another way, what realities of this leadership situation does a national leadership approach take into account that the pluralistic approach does not?

The national leadership approach acknowledges the possible impact of leadership interests on strategic arms decisions that would be taken into account by the pluralistic approach only if it could be shown that this impact resulted from the actual exertion of pressure (or even influence) on the leadership by some lower-level individuals or groups. However, since it cannot be ruled out that such interests would become manifest (or at least would be strengthened) as a consequence of the pressure of these individuals or groups, it is important to assess the extent to which the Soviet strategic arms decision-making setting appears to lend itself to pluralistic pressures within the overall context of an oligarchic political system.

Soviet Power Struggles

For present purposes, it is perhaps sufficient to note that, in broad terms, responsiveness by the top leaders to pressures from below is probably most likely in situations where there are sharp divisions in the ranks of the top leaders and they seek to use the support of particular Soviet institutions to wage their internecine battles—for example, the governmental apparatus, the party apparatus, the military, and the secret police. This is the stuff of which the famous Soviet power struggles over the years have been made.

Khrushchev's political career probably brought these power struggles into clearest relief in the postwar era as he turned for support first to one group and then to another to try to secure and maintain his ascendancy over the other Soviet leaders. Initially, he relied on the party apparatus as a whole to do battle with Malenkov, whose power base was in the governmental apparatus. Subsequently, he relied on regional party secretaries to undercut the economic role of the governmental apparatus and further weaken Malenkov and certain other key rivals. He was able to turn to the Soviet military in the person of Zhukov when the major showdown with those rivals came. He then apparently counted on the support of the Stalingrad group of Soviet military leaders in ousting Zhukov as minister of defense.

Khrushchev's success in the power struggles in the Kremlin in the 1950s is usually taken as a prime example of how Soviet leaders can and do cynically manipulate issues and policies to outflank their political opponents.[1] Khrushchev, for example, initially censured Malenkov's "soft line" in foreign and defense affairs and then later endorsed some of Malenkov's key positions (for example, on the destructiveness of nuclear war) when Malenkov had been subdued. Combined with the evidence of Khrushchev's adroitness in utilizing one group and then another to further his political career, this image of Soviet cynicism with respect to policy differences can create the impression that the top Soviet leaders are in fact little concerned with, or seriously beholden to, lower-level groups with particular interests to advance. Even if this image were correct on the whole, however it seems bound to be misleading in its particulars. Can it really be asserted that, say, at some point in Khrushchev's rise, when he looked to the support of the members of a given group, he would not have been susceptible to pressure from them on certain issues in which they were especially interested?

Such bitter political infighting is not an endemic Soviet condition, however. The current Soviet leadership, for example, seems to have agreed at some point that constant and vicious jockeying for power at the top can be profoundly destabilizing and detrimental to the interests of the regime as a whole. Differences among these leaders have been visible to Western observers, to be sure. Ousters from the top leadership ranks have been brought about by such differences (Podgorny and Shelepin, to name but two). And Brezhnev has maneuvered to make himself clearly pre-eminent. But at least until Podgorny's ouster in 1977, the post-Khrushchev leadership seems to have sustained a fairly strong commitment to the principle of collective rule, sufficient to mute the kind of infighting that would seem to offer the greatest opportunity for successful pressure from below.

In sum, as a first cut at the question of whether the Soviet political system lends itself to interest-group pressures on strategic arms decisions, it is important to avoid a generalization (even for the post-Stalin era) that betrays an insensitivity to differences in the nature and intensity of political jockeying in the top leadership circles over time.[2] If the decision in question occurs when such jockeying is particularly virulent, there would seem to be some chance that pressures from below have been heeded in making it. At other times, a decision that appears to violate what a rational strategic calculus would dictate may be more supportive of the assumptions of national leadership decision making— with the leaders being swayed by certain personal prefer- ences.

Pluralistic Elements in the Defense Sector

The basic considerations presented above rest on a premise that the pluralistic approach to Soviet defense decision making does not readily concede, that is, that Soviet defense decisions should not be arbitrarily separated from the broader context of Soviet politics. Since, however, the pluralistic interpretation could—without doing violence to its primary assumptions—take this broader context into account, the differences with the national leadership perspective are not fundamental on this score, although there still would be notable differences in how this broader political context would be treated.

For present purposes, the differences between the plural- istic interpretation and the national leadership approach that really matter lie in the treatment of heterogeneous elements within the defense setting. If the existence of the Supreme Defense Council and the phenomenon of five-year defense planning constitute the strong suit for a rational strategic actor point of view, the strong suit of the pluralistic point of view is simply the existence of a number of organizations in the defense sector that can be presumed to have particular strategic arms interests and considerable resources to promote them.

A pluralistic interpretation can cite, for example, the Ministry of Defense, whose minister is a member of the Supreme Defense Council (and a Politburo member), as an organization that should be capable of pressuring the top leaders to pursue policies favorable to the military in general versus policies that would favor civilian interests. At, strictly speaking, an even higher level of aggregation of defense interests, the Military Industrial Commission (VPK) would seem to provide a key forum for expression of the combined interests of the professional military and the defense industrial ministries as a whole.[3] As Raymond Garthoff has described it, this body "handles coordination between the Defense Ministry, ministries concerned with military production, and Academy of Sciences institutes engaged in military research and development."[4]

It is also pertinent to take into account organizations with a presumably more intense interest in specific weapon and defense policies. In this regard, one can cite the five military services under the Ministry of Defense and the eight (or more) defense industrial ministries (wherein weapon designers reside) that develop and produce weapons for the services.[5] Insofar as certain ministries tend to concentrate on weapons for certain services (for example, the Ministry of the Shipbuilding Industry for the Navy; the Ministry of General Machinebuilding for the Strategic Rocket Forces) a prima facie case could be made that these services and defense-industrial ministries combine efforts to shape particular weapons decisions.

Merely identifying such weapon systems interest groups does not suffice to prove that they are actually capable of pressuring the top leadership. But contrary arguments that rest consciously or unconsciously on the premises of the rational strategic actor approach are probably even less convincing. The very existence of the Supreme Defense Council probably constitutes the strongest counterargument. But even here, as we have seen, it cannot be ruled out that, even with its limited membership, the council would bear witness to top-level divisiveness, which lower-level groups could hope to exploit. The existence of five-year defense planning is probably the second strongest counterargument. But again, such planning may inhibit the successful exertion of lower-level pressure within a given plan period, but would certainly not rule it out as the plan is being shaped.

Another tack that it is tempting to take to deny the impact of lower-level pressures on top decision makers is to cite the special efforts that the Soviet leadership has made to exert tight control over defense production. There is no doubt that the Soviet leadership has tried valiantly to impose its will on the defense production effort over the years as a corollary to the according of high priority to that effort. At least until his promotion to the post of minister of defense, D.F. Ustinov served as the leadership's principal watchdog in this regard.[6] And he has been aided in this role by L.V. Smirnov, chairman of the Military Industrial Commission (VPK), and I.D. Serbin, chairman of the Defense Industry department of the Central Committee.

The effectiveness of the defense supervisors is easy to overstate, however. As studies of weapon systems decision making in the United States have demonstrated, the enormous technical complexities of modern weapon systems impose commensurate management burdens.[7] One should not lose sight of the fact that, whatever the peculiarities of their management approaches (and no matter how personally knowledgeable and diligent a person like Ustinov might be), the Soviets have probably not found a formula for avoiding some slack in top-level supervision of defense programs—especially when a variety of technologically complex weapon systems is in the works simultaneously. Nor can it be assumed that Ustinov, Smirnov, and Serbin have maintained a solid front against the importunities of weapon designers, defense industrial ministers, or service personnel. Indeed, while it can be presumed that these supervisors have basically agreed and worked well together, each has probably had substantial management resources at his individual disposal and (Ustinov's recent appointment aside) each has had a considerable tenure in his particular post. It would not be surprising therefore if these supervisors have been at odds on occasion and that such divisions have been apparent to the organizations and personnel they were supposed to supervise. In sum, it is not very convincing to base the case against the impact of pluralistic pressures on Soviet strategic arms decisions on an image of the top leaders and their principal agents behaving as if they were monolithic in their interests and superhuman in their capabilities.[8] One does not have to accept this image, however, to keep the possibilities for pluralistic defense decision making within reasonable bounds.

Both rational strategic actor and pluralistic approaches pay little attention to other features of the Soviet defense decision-making environment that are germane to an assessment of the impact of pluralistic pressures on Soviet strategic arms decisions. The existence of heterogeneous elements in the Soviet defense setting not only underpins the possibility for effective pluralistic pressure on strategic arms decisions, it may also help to impede it. This aspect of Soviet defense decision making is slighted by the rational strategic actor approach (because its assumptions deemphasize the significance of pluralistic elements in general) and by the pluralistic approach (because this aspect runs counter to the presumption of pluralistic impact). The national leadership decision-making perspective, however, with its emphasis on both the power of the top leaders and the relevance of heterogeneous elements, is quite congenial to the notion of pluralism in the service of central direction.

Paying heed to the broader realities of the Soviet defense setting in this case does not mean denying the relevance of those features of this setting that are given attention in the other approaches. It does mean that there are decision-making implications to be taken into account that put the assumptions of these other approaches in a wider perspective necessary to reflect more closely how the Soviet political system probably really operates.

In arguing the case for effective pluralistic pressure in

shaping Soviet strategic arms decisions, there is an
understandable tendency to focus on interest groups that
represent a relatively high level of interest aggregation—for
example, the military services. At that level of aggregation,
the presumption can fairly well be sustained that considerable resources can be mustered by the group to make an
impact on the Soviet leaders. In this regard, the case would
seem to be even better made if the combined interests of a
service and a defense-industrial ministry (acting as the
principal producer for the service) were emphasized. If one
probes deeper into this environment, however, questions are
prompted about such things as (1) the intensity of a given
military service's interest in a particular strategic weapon
system decision, (2) the intensity of a given defense industrial
ministry's interest in the decision, and (3) the congruence of
service and defense-industrial ministry interests. On the
service side, service-level interest in plumping for a
particular weapon system cannot be automatically presumed to be considerable just because the service would have
custody of the weapon. The service as a whole may have the
resources to promote the system actively if it so desires, but
the service's commitment could be much less than that of a
particular branch within the service. Pulling and hauling
within a service over weapon system priorities may be
virulent. Within the Ground Forces, for example, armor
partisans and artillery partisans could find themselves at
bitter odds in instances in which some choice has to be made
between the particular weapon system each desires. Similar
differences would seem likely between, say interceptor and
surface-to-air missile (SAM) advocates in the National
Aerospace Defense Forces (PVO) and between bomber and
fighter proponents in the Air Forces.

It is entirely possible that service-level backing would be
forthcoming that would be as strong as a program's original
supporters might wish. But it cannot be presumed out of
hand. This does not mean that a service would inevitably be

confronted with a difficult choice between competing weapon systems. There may be many cases in which no such choice has to be made. But if attention is paid to heterogeneous elements in the defense sector below the service level, it seems possible to argue that the interest of a service in promoting a given strategic weapon system may be less than a pluralistic approach might take for granted.

If one can err by assuming that service commitment to a weapon system is of an intensity that might be more likely found below the service level, a similar error is possible on the defense-industrial side of the equation. In that environment, commitment to a particular weapon program may be quite strong at the design-shop level—with a designer's interest in a given weapon system probably most closely approximating the intensity of interest likely to be shown at or below the service level. There have been cases of weapon designers successfully lobbying for a particular weapon system by gaining the ear of a top political leader.[9] But such efforts may exemplify personal impact on the part of the designers (rather than group pressure) at best. And indeed, it may be that the "success" of such efforts is more a reflection of the personal preference(s) of the leader than an indication of the persuasive powers of the designer.[10]

But what about the organizational resources the designer might muster to bring pressure to bear on the top leaders? A look at the production responsibilities of the defense-industrial ministries suggests that in many instances the support for a weapon system at the ministry level may be considerably less than a particular designer's commitment to it. In situations in which designers have to compete for the production of a new aircraft, for example, the minister of the Aviation Industry could count on producing the aircraft in his ministry no matter who won the competition. This competition might be for an aircraft for a particular service, say, the PVO. But the Ministry of the Aviation Industry develops and produces aircraft for other services—the Air

Forces and the Navy (Naval Aviation). In situations in which there may be a choice between going ahead with a new aircraft program for one of these services or the other (or the PVO), ministry-level concern with the outcome would seem to be less than that of either the designer or the services involved. In other words, one cannot presume that the interest in promoting a particular weapon system is as strong at the defense-industrial ministry level as it would be at the design-shop level or that there would be an inevitable congruence of interests between the service that would deploy a new weapon system and the defense-industrial ministry that would produce it.[11] Indeed, the possibility should not be excluded that, on occasion, a defense-industrial minister might try to block a new program.[12]

Basic Limits on Pluralistic Impact

For present purposes, this brief survey should suffice to indicate how, in many instances, the existence of heterogeneous elements in the Soviet defense sector might work to maintain centralized decision-making authority. To be sure, the Defense Council, five-year defense planning, and the basic diligence of the leadership's defense supervisors— which help to support the rational strategic actor approach—no doubt make a significant contribution to this end as well. But unless one takes into account what heterogeneity in the defense sector may accomplish in its own right, this contribution can easily get overstated to the point where unrealistic claims make a pluralistic approach seem credible by default.

Lower-level pressures on strategic arms decisions may be limited in two broad and complementary ways. First, the life might go out of the promotional effort for a weapon system simply in moving from the lowest levels of the military and defense industrial hierarchies, where the most interest in a program might be found, to the top. Accordingly, the top leaders may only occasionally be confronted with strong pressures for a weapon system from an interest group that represents a sufficient aggregation of interests to matter politically. Second, in light of the differences in the kinds of interests in the defense environment, the top leaders, either directly or, what is more likely, through the defense supervisors, may be able in many instances to frustrate the coalescence of support for particular programs.

The presumed ability of the defense supervisors (acting as the principal agents for the top leaders) to operate within this environment without necessarily going through channels, as it were, is probably of key importance here. The opportunities this may present for defense sector personnel (at various levels) to establish direct contact with the supervisors should not automatically be regarded as a pluralistic decision-making asset. Such contacts may enable these personnel to override or circumvent expected opposition at, say, the next formal level in their bureaucracy. But if the defense supervisors are directly accessible to designers, service personnel, and the like, so that differences among the supervisors can be exploited and the backing of at least one of them secured for some pet weapon program, those individuals are hardly less accessible to the defense supervisors so that pet programs can be frustrated by the supervisors. In short, this communication capability can be just as easily a liability as an asset for pluralistic decision making.

In general, the presumed wide-ranging access of the defense supervisors to personnel and organizations would seem likely to facilitate the top leadership's ability to exploit differences between and within services, defense-industrial ministries, design shops, and so on. Appreciation of the relevance of such differences suggests that the Soviet leaders and their principal agents do not have to be monolithic in their outlook and superhuman to boot, as a rational strategic actor approach would encourage one to believe, to stay on top of this situation much of the time. It also suggests that a pluralistic approach, while denying the monolithic nature of the Soviet regime, cannot confidently proceed on the tacit assumption that interest groups of potential political significance would themselves be monolithic.

In sum, this survey of some of the major features of the Soviet decision-making environment indicates that there are grounds for utilizing each of the three approaches that have been put forth. The national leadership approach calls attention to elements that help both underpin the other approaches and limit them. The premises of a rational strategic actor approach are basically supported by the existence of the Defense Council and mid-term defense planning—and by the role that pluralistic elements may play in helping to sustain centralized decision making. The premises of a pluralistic approach are basically supported by the existence of such consequential organizations as the armed services and the defense-industrial ministries—and by the limits to the role of the Defense Council and defense planning in fostering centralized decisions. And the premises of a national leadership approach are supported by the fact that the Defense Council and defense planning do not restrict the Soviet leaders to treating strategic arms decisions in a vacuum *and* that pluralistic elements in the defense setting can be used to frustrate lower-level pressure on the leadership. The Soviet decision-making environment therefore makes it possible for the Soviet leaders to make decisions on other than strategic grounds, but without necessarily succumbing to constituent pressure in doing so.

As has been pointed out, the peculiar circumstances in which a given decision (or set of decisions) takes place may offer clues as to which approach is likely to be nearest the mark in explaining the decision. A strategic arms decision of considerable significance from a national security standpoint and which bears the marks of mid-term defense planning could suggest that a rational strategic actor approach might be most useful. A decision having significant implications for service roles and missions and which occurs at a time of bitter infighting in the top leadership circles could indicate that a pluralistic interpretation might be particularly strong. A decision that is not readily explicable on strategic grounds but that has no great role and mission implications and takes place at a time of relative harmony in the leadership circles could be well explained in national leadership terms.

One must be wary, nonetheless, of regarding any such clues as sure guides to the selection of an approach. No matter how plausible any one approach may seem on its own, its plausibility can only be assured if it convincingly rules out the likelihood of other interpretations. And this cannot be done unless a substantial effort is made to utilize these approaches as well. Moreover, in doing so, it may well be found that in fact the most plausible explanation is really the combined product of all of them.

Part 3
Implications for the Present

6
Soviet Strategic Arms Decision-making Analyses and the Action-Reaction Phenomenon

For policymakers concerned with the Soviet strategic threat, knowledge of the operations of the Soviet defense decision-making environment can hardly be regarded as an end in itself. What ultimately matters, of course, are the Soviet strategic arms that emerge from this environment rather than the method by which the decisions are made that result in these weapons. Given the policymaker's priorities, it is tempting to discount the significance of decision-making analyses. To do so, however, would be to take a very narrow view of what constitutes the Soviet threat and what is necessary to assess it. The threat, after all, is composed of both Soviet intentions and Soviet capabilities. Since deciding on appropriate measures to deal with the threat may often call for some appreciation of the purposes behind the weapon systems that the United States has to contend with, decision-making analyses have a role to play. Indeed, in this respect, decision-making analyses are particularly relevant to the policymaker's concerns regarding the possible impact of U.S. arms programs on Soviet strategic behavior.

Capabilities and Intentions

Colin Gray has stated, "The details of who supported the arguments of the Strategic Rocket Forces' spokesmen and why, is far less significant than the fact that the Soviet Union will very soon have a large force of SS-19s deployed."[1]

Strictly speaking, this point of view is eminently reasonable. But on broader grounds, one can acknowledge the supreme salience of the Soviet strategic capabilities without branding all other aspects of the Soviet threat as trivial. Indeed, the motives behind those capabilities matter also. For more than a decade the Soviets have manifested a concern with the Chinese threat that seems based at least as much on the hostile intentions they attribute to the Chinese (or on their skepticism regarding Chinese sanity) as on a sober assessment of Chinese strategic capabilities. Similarly, while it is inconceivable that strategic capabilities such as the Soviets possess would ever be lightly regarded by U.S. policymakers, no matter who possessed them, surely their special significance derives from the antagonism the Soviet Union has shown toward the United States since World War II. If, however, this basic Soviet antagonism is taken for granted, it may seem possible to regard capabilities and intentions as somehow neatly separable. It would be simpler thus to focus on capabilities alone because, presumably, they really matter and they submit readily to hard evaluation.

Even a cursory look at one of the more recent capability acquisitions by the Soviets, however, suggests that confronting the question of Soviet intentions cannot be easily avoided and that it is not a trivial question. It has been argued, for example, that the Soviets now possess strike instruments (for example, ICBMs and submarine-launched ballistic missiles [SLBMs]) in sufficient quantity and quality for exercising limited strike options.[2] But the strike instruments themselves do not unambiguously indicate that the Soviets are seriously considering including plans for limited nuclear options in their overall strategic planning. The characteristics of the weapons could conform to the long-held (or long-touted) Soviet belief in the necessity to prepare for fighting—and winning—an all-out nuclear war.[3] Accordingly, that these weapons represent a limited options capability may be unintentional. They would still reflect a threat, to be sure, but not a genuine limited nuclear options threat. It is, however, obviously important for the United States to know what sort of threat (or threats) those strike instruments represent. As former Secretary of Defense Schlesinger has contended, the United States must seriously consider countermeasures to deal with this limited strike potential in any event, simply because the weapons could be used for limited strikes.[4] Yet in weighing the pros and cons of various U.S. courses of action with respect to such countermeasures, the question of Soviet intent must loom large. If one is convinced that the Soviets' limited nuclear options capability is a sufficient indicator of their intent to plan (or that they have inaugurated plans) for exercising those options, then one need not worry that U.S. actions might prompt the Soviets to commence such planning. On the other hand, if one is convinced that the Soviets are still hewing closely to professed doctrine (that is, that nuclear war will be all out) in their strategic planning, then it is at least open to question whether U.S. countermeasures (however prudent in the abstract) might become a self-fulfilling prophecy by helping to create a Soviet limited options threat.[5]

The point that matters here is that intentions and capabilities cannot be easily disentangled in terms of the hard choices that policymakers often have to make. The significance that is attached to particular capabilities that the Soviets have in hand (or that are discernible as being in the offing) at a given time will probably depend, to a considerable degree, on assumptions that are made either consciously or unconsciously about the Soviet motives behind those capabilities. And even if the general assumption regarding basic Soviet antagonism toward the United States is sustained, it hardly gives the policymaker very much to go on, as is illustrated above, in deciding on an appropriate course of action. Moreover, estimating future Soviet capabilities that the United States will have to deal with is very much a matter of determining the Soviet intent to achieve those capabilities.

Thus, since it may prove important for policymakers to know more than that the Soviet Union is about to acquire or has acquired a particular capability, analyzing Soviet strategic arms decision making may be a worthwhile enterprise. No easy or simple answers are likely to be forthcoming, but at least in considering the significance of Soviet capabilities it can help one to progress beyond making general or unconscious assumptions about the Soviet intentions behind those capabilities. Progress in this regard is especially important—as indicated by the limited nuclear options example—when the policymaker has particular reason to consider whether and how U.S. actions will affect Soviet behavior.

Decision-making Analyses and the Role of the Action-Reaction Phenomenon

Against the backdrop of the preceding discussion, it bears emphasizing that whatever general brief can be made on behalf of adding the national leadership approach to the repertoire of interpretations of Soviet strategic arms decision making, the approach does not hold out the promise of stripping away the difficulties of gauging the impact of the action-reaction phenomenon on Soviet strategic arms decisions. Indeed, in some ways it may add to those difficulties or at least make them more apparent.

To what extent do actions by the United States prompt

Soviet reactions in strategic arms policies and weapon programs? The answer will presumably vary from case to case. But it will also presumably vary according to the mode of analysis employed in a particular case. At first glance, in roughly conforming to one of the two broad schools of thought on the strategic arms race described earlier, a rational strategic actor approach would generally emphasize the role of the international action-reaction phenomenon in shaping Soviet strategic arms decisions. A pluralistic interpretation, on the other hand, would appear to generally deemphasize it.

The apparent difference between these approaches rests on assumptions about the locus of decision-making power and the motives (or perceptions) that might reasonably be attributed to the relevant decision makers. Assuming that decision-making power would be held tightly in the hands of one or a few top leaders and that decisions would be made with a keen perception of strategic realities, the rational strategic actor approach suggests that Soviet strategic arms decisions would be highly sensitive to actions of the USSR's principal strategic rival.[6]

Pluralistic interpretations, on the other hand, are based on the notion that relevant decision-making power may be effectively shared by organizations and individuals below the top political level. Because these organizations and individuals are presumed to seek to shape defense decisions out of motives that are only incidental to "objective" Soviet strategic needs, their sensitivity to U.S. actions is not likely to be high. Of course, it might be argued, it cannot be ruled out that a decision shaped by such lower-level influence would appear to Western observers as a reasonable Soviet response to some U.S. action. Moreover, it cannot be ruled out that a U.S. action would be taken into account by those pushing parochial interests if only because it could help them sell a weapon system idea to the top decision makers.

The Rational Strategic Actor Approach

Although, in general, the rational strategic actor approach would appear supportive of the impact of the action-reaction phenomenon and the pluralistic approach unsupportive, there are complicating considerations to be taken into account. In the first place, if one pays heed to the role of five-year defense planning, which seems important to help make the case for rational strategic actor defense decision making in the Soviet Union, responsiveness to U.S. actions would seem somewhat inhibited. Obviously, U.S. actions that were regarded as particularly significant and that occurred within a planning cycle could be taken into account if the Soviet leaders were willing to disrupt the plan to do so. But, in general, given the existence of a five-year plan, high responsiveness would seem to be confined to the period when the next plan was being considered and priorities were being decided. Thus, U.S. actions that occurred within this period (that is, anywhere from several months to a year or more before the inauguration of the next plan) would be most likely to have impact on Soviet defense decisions. Earlier U.S. actions could, of course, also elicit a response at this time, but the response would, by definition, be tardy.

Another complicating consideration that is inherent in the rational strategic actor approach is the difficulty of defining the strategic values (that is, in the strict military sense) that are appropriate for estimating Soviet responsiveness in a particular case. Insofar as these strategic values may be a combination of the common and the peculiar that could vary over time and from case to case, determining the role of the action-reaction phenomenon is likely to be more complicated than if it could be flatly assumed that the Soviets shared U.S. strategic values or that they did not. As a consequence, the role of the action-reaction phenomenon might easily be overstated or understated. Placing too much emphasis on the peculiarity of Soviet strategic values in a given instance could, for example, lead one to conclude that the Soviets had not responded to some U.S. action when in fact they had done so (or vice versa). A similar possibility for misgauging Soviet responsiveness could result from over-stressing the significance of strategic values the Soviets might hold in common with the United States. In short, while acknowledging the need to be sensitive both to peculiar Soviet strategic values and those the Soviets may share with the United States the rational strategic actor approach does not and cannot offer any sure guide for determining what the particular mix of these values might be in shaping a given Soviet strategic arms effort, and, in turn, the role of the action-reaction phenomenon.

The Pluralistic Approach

Soviet decisions that can be plausibly explained on pluralistic grounds may reflect the operation of the action-reaction phenomenon in a more genuine way than one would at first suspect. That lower-level organizations or individuals may use evidence of some U.S. action to sell their particular program should not be written off as merely incidental to the more basic fact that the pertinent Soviet decision was shaped by narrow bureaucratic motives. To serve their purposes, services, designers, and others might be inclined to bend the evidence to make the case for their desired weapon program. But does this mean that the action-reaction phenomenon really counts for little? Soviet decisions may be shaped by pluralistic pressures and yet reflect a genuine responsiveness to U.S. actions.

It is easy to overstate the selfishness of motive and the narrowness of perception that might characterize defense decisions shaped by pluralistic pressures. Even if it is conceded that those with the greatest stakes in a particular decision would have that interest no matter what the "real" significance of a U.S. action might be for the Soviets strategically, they presumably have to deal with individuals and organizations at higher levels who at best may have a weaker selfish interest in the decision. Thus, there may be a limiting factor at work. The probability of success may be greater for those programs that are promoted by means of a serious and convincing concern for the strategic implications for the Soviet Union of the U.S. action.

This does not mean that Soviet decisions that resulted from such pluralistic pressures would invariably make good sense from an overall strategic standpoint (whether by U.S. or Soviet standards). But if it is reasonable to suppose that programs would have a better chance of being sold to officials at the top of the military and political hierarchies if those officials could be convinced they made good sense, then chances are that (1) decisions that were, in fact, made as a consequence of pluralistic pressures could well reflect genuine responsiveness to U.S. actions, and (2) those decisions in many instances might not be all that different from those the Soviet leadership might make as a rational strategic actor.

There is nothing here to rule out the possibility that Soviet decisions may be shaped by pluralistic pressures when no particular U.S. deployment effort or action in the international arena is in evidence. Indeed, this possibility is crucial to the underlying assumption of a pluralistic approach that weapon programs tend to be self-generating, prompted largely by internal pressures rather than competition with an international adversary. This includes the notion of the technological imperative or, as Herbert York has described it in assessing U.S. weapon decision-making, the phenomenon of, in effect, running an arms race with oneself.[7] Even if the enemy has not, in fact, demonstrated a specific technological capability in some weapon area, one's own discovery of the feasibility of an achievement in that area prompts efforts to push ahead in the expectation that he will. A determination of the operation of this phenomenon on the Soviet side over the years would first require pinpointing those cases in which a Soviet technological lead was discerned and in which the United States came in a decided second or had chosen not to race at all. Only then would it be prudent to make an evaluation of whether the technological imperative led to specific Soviet strategic arms decisions as a consequence of pluralistic pressures.

A pluralistic approach seems particularly congenial to reflecting the impact of the technological imperative because it is at the lower levels of the defense establishment hierarchy that the greatest sensitivity to new technological possibilities is likely to be found. This pertains to research scientists and weapon designers, in particular, and key personnel in the services (affiliated with service-level technical organizations[8]) with whom designers can be expected to have regular contacts. Even given a reasonable presumption of enthusiasm on the part of these personnel for pushing forward the frontiers of technology in some weapon area, mitigating considerations should be taken into account. Memoir material—and analyses done on the basis of that material—have tended, for example, to stress the basic conservatism of Soviet weapon designers at least until recently.[9] In addition, weapon system ideas that are technologically adventurous may meet with considerable opposition at higher levels in the defense establishment hierarchy. Defense-industrial ministers, for example, may be particularly wary because developing and producing such weapons could involve them in unwanted dependencies on other defense-industrial ministries and the Academy of Sciences and, in general, increase their management burdens.[10] By the same token, it is unlikely that the top leadership would be kept in the dark about a technologically adventurous program until a promotional effort for it had achieved considerable organizational momentum. Through their defense supervisors (that is, Ustinov, Smirnov, Serbin,

and their subordinates), the top leadership would probably
be apprised early on of technologically promising weapon
prospects discovered in the design shops and laboratories.

These considerations suggest that the impact of the
peculiar action-reaction phenomenon embodied in the
technological imperative may be difficult to determine in
terms of its probable reflection in a specific decision-making
approach. A pluralistic approach could well be particularly
sensitive to the operation of a technological imperative in
Soviet strategic arms decisions. But the Soviet leadership
could function as a rational strategic actor and accommodate the notion of a technological imperative as well.
Having been apprised of certain promising weapon
prospects by their defense supervisors, the Soviet leadership
could decide for the systems' development and deployment
on the grounds of strict strategic calculation without being
pressured in any significant way by interested parties.

The National Leadership Approach

The national leadership approach can be expected to
further complicate efforts to judge the role of the action-
reaction phenomenon in Soviet strategic arms decisions. In
the first place, in emphasizing the significance of the
personal preferences of the top Soviet leaders, the national
leadership approach is also amenable to taking into account
the impact of the peculiar action-reaction phenomenon
embodied in the notion of a technological imperative. As
noted earlier, a designer may on his own make a case to one
(or more) of the top leaders on behalf of a new weapon
system. It may be that the personal biases of the leader (or
leaders) toward the designer himself, toward the kind of
system he is advocating, or toward the service that would
deploy it would be the determining factor in deciding to give
the go ahead for the system. But, as also noted, this
action-reaction phenomenon may be more in the nature of a
self-generating force for weapon efforts than a manifestation

of real international interaction.

At the same time, however, a Soviet strategic arms decision that could be convincingly explained on national leadership grounds could reflect a type of reaction to a U.S. action that would tend to be overlooked or downgraded in other approaches. To be sure, a reaction that was largely the product of national leadership decision making could share some characteristics of rational strategic actor or pluralistic pressure decisions—for example, if the relevant personal preferences of the top leaders were basically military preferences (for a particular service, or designer, or kind of weapon system).

But the national leadership approach also makes particular allowance for the impact on decisions of other preferences by the top leaders that could lie outside the military domain. Acting as national leaders, the Soviet leadership could respond to a U.S. action by shaping a strategic arms decision to serve broad political values. Considerations such as general prestige or political leverage in the world at large or in a particular region could impinge heavily on a Soviet strategic arms decision.

This is not the place to try to identify the nonmilitary values of the Soviet leadership that might shape a strategic arms response to a U.S. action. Leaders like Brezhnev, Kosygin, and (until his political demise) Podgorny, who can be expected to have a general concern for the Soviet Union's international standing (and who are Supreme Defense Council members), would likely be attentive to the wider foreign policy implications of strategic arms decisions. Foreign Minister Andrei Gromyko is not a Supreme Defense Council member, but his membership in the Politburo since April 1973 would increase the chances that broad foreign policy concerns would affect Soviet strategic arms decisions, at least when those decisions reach the Politburo.[11] (Furthermore, as Garthoff has noted, Gromyko may be called upon to attend Supreme Defense Council meetings on

occasion.[12]) Finally, individuals such as Mikhail Suslov and
Boris Ponomarev, who presumably have a particular interest
in ideological matters (both domestic and international),
could also bring this concern to Politburo deliberations of
strategic arms decisions and influence them accordingly. As
a consequence of these various leadership concerns, strategic
arms decisions could result that, while responsive to certain
U.S. actions, would be somewhat different from what the
Soviet professional military might seek or U.S. analysts
expect.[13]

It may be objected that one does not have to adopt the
national leadership decision-making approach to appreciate the importance of these broader political values in
shaping Soviet strategic arms decisions. In examining Soviet
concerns in the strategic arms limitation talks [SALT] (particularly SALT I), for example, Western analysts have noted
the apparent premium the Soviets have placed on achieving
agreements that make them appear to be as powerful as (or
perhaps even more powerful than) the United States in the
eyes of the world.[14] Similarly, in examining the limited
strike options possibilities of the emerging Soviet strategic
offensive weapons, there has been at least implicit concern
with the potential political leverage that might accrue to the
Soviets, particularly in dealing with Western Europe, by
being perceived to have a limited options capability.[15]

The foregoing examples suggest that Western observers
have not been insensitive to concerns that go beyond strict
military calculation that may shape Soviet strategic arms
decisions. Yet it is one thing to take these concerns into
account and quite another to explain how those concerns
can come to impact on Soviet strategic arms decisions. As
presently construed at any rate, the pluralistic approach does
not seem capable of indicating effectively how broad
political concerns can shape a Soviet defense decision. Even
if one concedes that lower-level promotion of a particular
decision may require more than perfunctory treatment of

strategic realities, such treatment would still probably be framed in fairly strict military terms. This is a consequence of the environment in which the promotional effort takes place. A designer or a service partisan for some new system is not likely to try to gain support from Ministry of Defense officials or defense-industrial ministers by stressing, for example, the significance a new system might have in increasing Soviet political leverage in Europe. Rather, the argument is likely to be made on the grounds that the new system would give the Soviet Union some specific military advantage.[16]

In the case of rational strategic actor interpretations, the impact of broader Soviet political concerns in shaping defense decisions is also not likely to receive appropriate treatment. To be sure, since the calculations of the top leaders are made paramount in this mode of analysis these broader concerns could be conceded some role. But in doing so, it would be very difficult to maintain the primacy that this approach accords strict strategic calculation in shaping Soviet strategic arms decisions and the basic organizational assumptions upon which this primacy depends—namely the essential separation of defense and civilian decision making. Accordingly, it seems that a national leadership decision-making approach, which emphasizes the decision-making power of the top Soviet leaders and their suscepti-bility to preferences that extend beyond the strictly military, would have the greatest sensitivity to broader political concerns and, what is equally important, the capability to indicate their impact in a logically consistent manner.[17]

Responding to the Soviet Threat: A Cautionary Note

In sum, depending on the approach one finds most con-genial in explaining a Soviet strategic arms decision, the international action-reaction phenomenon may be given more or less emphasis. But no single approach is likely to have a monopoly on giving proper attention to this phenomenon. In general, the rational strategic actor approach may give more attention to it than the other approaches, but a Soviet strategic arms decision that might be explained plausibly on pluralistic grounds could also register the impact of a discrete U.S. action, as could a decision that was explicable on the basis of a national leadership approach. What this survey indicates above all is that Soviet responses to U.S. actions may be much more difficult to pin down than is commonly assumed and that the best way to gauge the role of the action-reaction phenomenon in a given Soviet strategic arms decision is to try to analyze that decision from more than one decision-making perspective.

For the present, this suggests the need for considerable caution in evaluating the Soviet strategic threat and what the United States should do about it. On the one hand, by indicating that in many ways a Soviet reaction to a U.S. action might be highly complex and not readily discernible even after the fact (much less predictable beforehand), the foregoing analysis argues for a wary attitude toward assuming that a U.S. action (for example, in a strategic arms program) would not ultimately redound to the detriment of U.S. security. On the other hand, the foregoing analysis equally does not support a contrary assumption.

In general, the implications of the study, given its basically preliminary nature, do not fall readily into the categories of hard-line or soft-line estimates of Soviet strategic intentions. To be sure, stressing the need to pay more analytical attention to the personal concerns or preferences of the Soviet leaders as national leaders, for example, could lead one to emphasize factors, such as Soviet civilian economic programs, that would seem contrary to the notion that Soviet strategic arms priorities would be likely to win through in the years ahead. But by the same token, this same analytical emphasis could wind up encouraging identification of leadership preferences, with respect to particular military services or the broader international politico-strategic utility of strategic arms programs, for instance, that could make Soviet strategic arms priorities seem particularly strong. In this regard, to the extent that it is possible to identify Soviet hawks and doves (and the study as a whole implicitly suggests this may be much more difficult to do than we tend to assume), analysis of a particular arms decision might unexpectedly suggest that the hawkish concern to push the program would be greater in the top political circles than in the Ministry of Defense. The basic point to be stressed, however, is that while future analyses may improve our understanding of these matters, it is decidedly premature at this juncture to expect Soviet defense decision-making analyses to offer any firm conclusions about present or future Soviet strategic intentions.

Part 4
Multiple Approaches and
Future Analyses

Introduction to Part 4

As stated in the introduction, this study only begins what ideally would be a very large analytic effort. A substantial appreciation of the strengths and weaknesses of our assumptions about how and why certain Soviet strategic arms decisions are made—and hence an improvement in our understanding of those decisions—basically requires a series of individual decision-making case studies. Even then we are unlikely to have a real key to the mysteries of Soviet strategic behavior. But only then will we be in a position to make anything approaching a reasonably firm statement on the utility of particular approaches for the analyst and the policymaker he informs. Only then will we be able to classify Soviet strategic arms decisions in the sort of detail that would even begin to approximate a true taxonomy. For such detail should include, to the extent possible, a matchup of particular categories of strategic arms decisions and particular Soviet decision-making practices.

If, as most social (and other) scientists agree, classification is near the bottom rung of the ladder of scientific understanding and prediction perhaps at the top, we are at best just beginning the climb. To pretend otherwise may not only be dangerous, because of the security stakes involved, but may also keep us from doing the spadework without which no real progress is likely to be made. And such spadework would profitably include subjecting individual Soviet strategic arms decisions (or sets of decisions) to analysis along multiple lines of inquiry.

It is recognized, however, that even though the approaches presented in this study cast doubt on some of the longstanding assumptions about the role of the international action-reaction phenomenon, the utility of these approaches may still be questioned. After all, judgments are being made every day about Soviet strategic arms programs and policies without much evident use of explicit decision-making approaches. And it may well seem that, rather than helping us to come to grips with a basic data problem, a decision-making outlook simply causes serious data problems to arise.

It is the particular purpose of the concluding chapters of this study, therefore, to show that for a variety of reasons the overall data problem in analyzing Soviet strategic arms decisions may be less apparent than it should be and that, while decision-making approaches cannot wish that problem away, they can, in fact, be put to use to help us to better understand and cope with it.

7
Appreciating the Data Problem: Sources of Obscurity

It is hardly a revelation that we have much less information than we would like about Soviet weapons efforts and defense policies upon which our very lives may depend. Yet the full implications of this deficiency can easily be obscured. We can get into the habit of thinking about these matters in ways that leave many basic assumptions unchallenged and result in an analytic landscape littered with contradictions. Consider, for example, the chances of having the data problem itself invoked against both an explicit decision-making approach to some Soviet weapon program and an interpretation of the program whose decision-making assumptions were merely implicit. It would be no surprise to find that those who were the sternest skeptics in the former case would accept rather extensive decision-making assumptions in the latter case with utter equanimity.

The Impact of Policy Needs

One of the reasons for such inconsistent treatment of the data problem is that the needs of scholarship and the needs of policy do not neatly coincide. Indeed, the aspect of Soviet life

that Western policymakers most need to have clearly
illuminated is the most opaque part for scholars. It is
sobering to realize that if assessing Soviet strategic arms
efforts were but an academic concern, and if rigorous
standards of social science inquiry were the sole guide as to
whether and how to address the problem, sheer avoidance
might be the most prudent course of action. Since the needs
of policy do not permit such discretion, however, it would
seem necessary for the analyst to be at least as rigorous a
social scientist as possible under the circumstances.

But if the requirements of policy oblige attention, in the
first place, to an area of inquiry that might otherwise best be
ignored, they can also intrude on the analyst's ability to
function as a scholar. The need for a relatively rapid
response to immediate policy problems, for example, can
easily compress one's time horizon in looking at Soviet
strategic arms decisions and cause one to focus mainly on
near-term events with perhaps but a brief nod to the past.
Now, quite obviously legitimate policy needs would not be
served if analysts adopted the frame of mind of the
apocryphal character who gave the history of meteorology
whenever he was asked about the day's weather. But such a
reordering of analytical priorities seems unlikely.[1]

Even for a relatively limited analysis, a serious look at the
past seems in order. For example, in seeking to interpret the
significance of some new Soviet weapon system, doesn't it
make sense at least to try to investigate the context in which
the original decisions on that program were probably taken?
The possibility clearly exists that the system could acquire a
bona fide strategic rationale only as it reaches initial
operational capability (IOC). Clearly, too, levels and kinds
of deployment could be determined by factors that characterize the present international setting. But unless one assumes
the existence of a marvelously clairvoyant Soviet political
and military leadership when the program got going, it
seems pertinent to take into account such questions as the

following: What concerns *at the time* would have affected the Soviets' appreciation of their weapon system needs? What, for example, would have been a reasonable projection on their part *at the time* of the threat with which they would have to contend in the future? What would have affected their estimate, *at the time*, of particular deficiencies in the Soviet force posture that needed to be remedied?[2]

In a broader sense, giving the past short shrift simply means that conclusions will be drawn and generalizations will be made on the basis of much less data than are really available. Without taking those data deliberately into account, we have no way of knowing whether they are "good" or "bad", whether they would support or undermine these conclusions and generalizations. What we can recognize, however, is that in adhering to a basically ahistorical perspective, we are in fact compounding the data problem with which Soviet strategic arms decisions confront us in the first place. That we may be inclined to make do with this situation, when faced with the need to explain arms programs of such great significance to our security, must derive at least in part from a kind of basic confusion—the belief that to respond to immediate policy needs our analytical focus must be similarly immediate.[3]

A complementary factor that works to obscure the data problem in analyzing Soviet strategic arms decisions is the premium placed on narrow specialization. Given the complexities involved, it would be ridiculous to claim that particular kinds of expertise are not required. It would be equally silly to argue that the premium placed on specialization is solely the result of the demand of policy. Nevertheless, such specialization is reinforced by the institutional frameworks that have been established to provide policy-makers with expert advice on Soviet strategic arms efforts. And while specialization is necessary to deal with the data problem, it can also frustrate efforts to cast the data net widely to get more and different information and encourage practices that mask the need even to do so.

There is, for example, the understandable temptation for analysts to stack the cards in favor of their own field of specialization and then at best tack on a caveat or simply an addendum from some other field to convince themselves and others that their analysis has been appropriately broad-gauged. In a more sophisticated fashion, the semblance of a broad-gauged, methodologically coherent interpretation of some Soviet strategic arms program can be created by simply pulling together, and perhaps juggling, the conclusions reached in a number of narrow analyses that have been pursued independently. This effort is better than making no attempt at all at integrating diverse sorts of expertise, but it can be counterproductive if it leads to the conviction that the constraints of specialization have really been overcome.

There are two (somewhat less defensible) tendencies that are also nurtured by specialization. There is the urge to batten down the intellectual hatches when faced with the possibility that areas outside one's own expertise are germane to a problem and to dismiss those areas out of hand—without even cursory investigation of their relevance. A variant of this tendency is to acknowledge the possible relevance of certain factors that are beyond the pale of one's expertise and then systematically ignore them when conclusions are offered. For example, many would probably be willing to acknowledge that, although largely unknown, how the Soviets actually decide on strategic arms programs is an element that is relevant to our interpretation of, say, Soviet intentions. Having conceded this, however, do we not frequently reach conclusions (based on our reading of what may be relatively knowable with regard to these programs, such as weapon characteristics) in which this decision-making unknown has simply been factored out[4]—a case of validity by omission?[5]

By the same token, specialization can result in analyses that are insidious in that elements that are appendages—

albeit crucial appendages—to a main body of solid scholarly investigation are given more respectability than they deserve. This phenomenon is most prevalent in cases where cursory and largely unsupported social science judgments can be married to impressive physical science analyses of some Soviet strategic arms program to produce an overall interpretation that can appear quite convincing. This sort of effort is probably not the product of any deliberate methodological sleight of hand, but may be the result more of a certain defensiveness the social sciences have manifested, especially in recent years. When respectability in the social sciences has come to be associated with the ability to sport the trappings of the physical sciences, it is not to be wondered that in analyses that really do contain a large chunk of solid physical science investigation the social science component should be able to bask in reflected glory.

Another setting in which this claim to validity by extension can find expression is in broad studies of the cold war, in which Soviet strategic arms programs may be treated more or less indirectly. It is tempting to take what may be very diligent work on the American side of the equation as sufficient indication that a valid case has been made for the Soviet side as well. To be sure, the specialization reflected in such efforts is probably more likely to be found outside the institutional frameworks established to provide policy-makers with professional advice on Soviet strategic arms efforts—and indeed would tend to be reinforced by the lack of access to classified data consequential to being on the outside. But it is a form of specialization, nonetheless, and can readily contribute to the tendency to lose sight of the formidable data problems involved in fathoming Soviet strategic arms decisions.

This discussion is not meant to suggest that the problem involved in analyzing Soviet strategic arms programs and policies is merely one of looking where the light is. Strictly speaking, what else can one do but look at what can be seen?

And even with a windfall of data from some Soviet official with a high rank and a large packing case, the most diligent historical and/or multidisciplinary investigation still could not explicate fully the whys and wherefores of Soviet strategic arms decisions. The problem rather is that the demands of policy can encourage us to believe that we see much more of the analytical landscape than we really do and that therefore there is no real need to try to illuminate more of it.

Habits in Viewing the Soviets

It may also be difficult to appreciate the implications of the data problem in analyzing Soviet strategic arms decisions because of the influence of a certain frame of reference that one can easily adopt in thinking in general about things Soviet. This mind-set takes its cue from Churchill's famous remark about Russia: "It is a riddle wrapped in a mystery inside an enigma; but perhaps there is a key. That key is Russian national interest." While the prose is expert, the methodological message is not exactly conducive to sound analysis. Indeed, that message may be downright pernicious, leading us to believe that so long as we have forthrightly conceded the existence of a basic data problem in dealing with the USSR, the problem really doesn't have to stand in our way.

Consider the contradiction Churchill's message contains. On the one hand, there is the apparent admission that we have much less to go on—doubtless because of Soviet secretiveness, among other things—in trying to understand the behavior of this particular state than is the case with other countries. On the other hand, there is the suggestion that nevertheless a key to understanding can somehow be found. The validity of using national interest as a key is not at issue here. What is at issue is the very legitimacy of the hope of finding a key—any key—under the circumstances.

If, by any reasonably strict definition, real keys to the behavior of countries or individuals can be found, they are more likely to turn up in situations where good and plentiful data permit the kind of rigorous analysis that will yield valid generalizations, and not where such analysis admittedly cannot easily be done. And yet it would not be surprising to find that the tendency to think in terms of keys to understanding, whether explicitly labeled as such or merely reflected implicitly in sweeping single-factor explanations, is more pronounced in our inquiry into Soviet behavior than in our research on, say, the French, Germans, or ourselves. In any event, what matters is that that sort of thinking is likely to be regarded as most acceptable in the Soviet case— precisely where it is, in fact, least supportable from a methodological standpoint.

Many factors combine to make it appear quite acceptable to satisfy the analyst's natural urge to generalize in treating the Soviets. The most basic factor would seem to be that we have gotten used to thinking about the USSR as a special state to which it is appropriate to apply correspondingly special research techniques in order to gain necessary insights. This is not intended to deny that in important respects the USSR *is* special or to denigrate the contribution that even the most arcane Kremlinological investigation might yield; it is simply to suggest that ultimately our analytical efforts must be judged by more basic standards of inquiry.

Overstressing the peculiarity of the Soviets and the techniques that have been developed to comprehend them, however, can cause us to lose sight of the fact that we resort to these techniques in the first place largely because of data deficiencies that keep us from pursuing the kinds of analyses that are feasible elsewhere—and that should more readily yield valid generalizations. It may well be contended, of course, that shortcutting broader data requirements in analyzing the Soviets is not only necessary but also quite

legitimate methodologically because the genuinely special
nature of the Soviet system permits it. While to some extent
this may be true, there is a very real danger here of becoming
ensnared in a tautology. Treatment of the Soviet ideology
offers a case in point. Given the overall data problem we
confront in analyzing the Soviets, it would be wonderfully
convenient if the articulated ideology could be relied upon as
a guide to Soviet behavior, thus sparing us the grim labors
we must endure in trying to fathom the behavior of other
states—states that may embarrass us with data riches but
refuse to accommodate us with blueprints.[6] We can, to be
sure, go a long way toward convincing ourselves that we
have this convenience by making the assumption (however
hazy) that one of the things that makes the USSR special is
the role of ideology. It is then only a few short steps to a chain
of reasoning that starts with the premise that it is legitimate
to regard the articulated ideology as a reliable guide to Soviet
behavior, because the USSR is special, and ends with the
USSR being proved special, because, among other things,
the articulated ideology can be shown to be a reliable guide
to its behavior!

What permits such a tautology to be sustained is that it is
relatively easy to pick and choose from Soviet ideological
pronouncements (as the Soviets appear to do themselves, in a
kind of Hallmark card approach to events) to find a suitable
ideological explanation for their behavior in a particular
situation. And once one has entered into the spirit of things,
then it can appear that basic methodological requirements
are met simply by amassing quotations.

There are two notable contradictions in this situation. For
one thing, it is curious, to say the least, that the articulated
ideology can, in effect, be treated as a kind of iron hand
guiding Soviet actions (even to the point of Lenin's
pronouncements being regarded as the handbook of a master
programmer) when there might not have been a Soviet state
in the first place if the Bolsheviks had not seen fit to

accommodate the ideology to reality.

Second, if we can take the Soviets at their ideological word, it is curious that one rarely sees (except, perhaps, in the case of outright apologists for the regime) any citation of the flattering remarks that glut the Soviet litany—about the glories of Soviet society, the USSR's dedication to peace, and so on. Presumably they are rare because, even when analysts might be inclined to pick contrary quotations to argue about specific Soviet foreign or defense policies, there is broad agreement that such pronouncements should simply be written off as unbelievable. But this is a position that is hardly consistent with the underlying assumption that Soviet ideological pronouncements themselves can serve "independently" as a means to test our hypotheses about Soviet behavior in particular cases.[7] And if that is so, then it surely casts doubt on the sensibility of viewing one's methodological chores as nearly complete when a thick stack of quotations has been assembled.[8]

The point here is not that the articulated Soviet ideology has no analytical utility. Rather, it is that we can all too easily succumb to the temptation to use it as a short cut to understanding, absolving us from the necessity of grappling with the kinds of subtle and complex interpretive problems that regularly confront us in dealing with the behavior of other states. In short, because the ideology is palpably different from the ideologies of at least most non-Communist states in certain respects (for example, in being set down in black and white as official) and because it seems to promise a way to make up for inadequate data in comprehending Soviet actions, one can lose sight of the fact that it is itself preeminently a part of the problem of understanding the Soviets and not by any means a ready-made solution. We can begin to appreciate that fact if we but consider that if deficiencies in data make it appealing to look to Soviet ideological pronouncements for guidance in the first place, there is also a very good chance that these same deficiencies will make it difficult to determine how reliable that guidance might be.[9]

There are other aspects of the way we tend to view things Soviet that reflect the urge to simplify—or to mask—what in other cases would be regarded as formidable analytical problems. Our desire to get the big answers to the big questions about the USSR can encourage us to give patient and respectful audience to ruminations about the Soviets that, through sheer repetition, appear much more solidly grounded than they are—or could possibly be. It may make some sense, for example, for Western policymakers to worry more about the "ultimate" foreign policy goals of the USSR than about those of other states. Yet repeated expressions of that concern cannot somehow facilitate recognition of those ultimate goals—if indeed there really are any.[10] It can only create the impression that what we would be likely to regard as a well nigh impossible analytical task elsewhere, where the data are comparatively richer, can be (or has been) accomplished in the case of the Soviets.

That such ruminations about where the Soviets are going can get a respectful hearing may be reinforced by a certain tolerance we may have developed for similar ruminations about where the Soviets have been and what it means for their present behavior. Since even the most elementary course in cultural anthropology is hardly required to point out that there are various complex mixes of similarities and differences among the peoples of the earth, it says something about our approach to things Soviet that we should be somewhat less than comfortable with the notion of the Soviets fitting into this pattern. Perhaps it is our concern with our ability to predict Soviet actions that tempts us to reduce the Soviets to, on the one hand, a nation of cloned Americans (if not yet perhaps fully developed) or, on the other hand, a nation of totally alien—indeed, unearthly— beings. Clearly, no one can be expected to own up to subscribing to such fantasies. Yet how far from them can we really be if, for example, we latch onto some single factor in the Russian experience—such as the peasant past—as a means to establish and explain that the current Soviet leadership brings unique attitudes about the role of violence and coercion to its deliberations on, say, strategic nuclear weapons.[11]

A final notable aspect of our habits of viewing things Soviet is our concern for who is up and who is down in the Kremlin: Whose career is on the rise? Whose is on the downslide? Who is in favor and who is out? Who will succeed whom? As bizarre as some of the means of making such determinations might seem to the uninitiated (such as noting who stands where on reviewing stands), those means have proved useful and, what is more, the concern behind them is eminently reasonable—and would be in the case of any country in which the United States was interested. But our particular preoccupation with this concern in the Soviet case can lead us to lose sight of something at least equally important.

Protocol considerations aside, predicting who will succeed whom is not an end in itself. Indeed, it really matters only if we can get a reasonable understanding of whether the successor will be different in terms of the policies he will pursue. Such an understanding is, of course, difficult enough to obtain in analyzing American politics, where there is a lot for the analyst to go on. The data problem in the Soviet case means utilizing informed guesswork at best.[12] Yet focusing on the mere fact of the change in personnel in the USSR can serve to create the impression that one's analytical tasks are nearly complete when in fact they are only just beginning—and indeed may not in any meaningful sense be possible at all.

Method Mystiques in the Social Sciences

In addition to the press of policy and the influence

(admittedly, not always direct) of some of the habits that have been cultivated in our thinking in general about things Soviet, a third basic factor would seem to play a part in impeding our appreciation of the data problems we confront in analyzing Soviet strategic arms decisions. That factor is the tendency, perhaps all too widespread in the social sciences nowadays, to confuse methodological responsibility and respectability with the ability to construct a general theory—or, more particularly, some elaborate model—to serve as the encompassing and exclusive means of dealing with certain broad categories of social science phenomena. Since the use of multiple approaches in the present study has been advocated to show that there is perhaps a more appropriate way to be methodologically responsible and respectable in treating Soviet strategic arms decisions, only a few cursory observations on the topic seem warranted here.

As a brief reminder of how what may be an acceptable way of going about our business in a data-rich setting may be counterproductive in a data-poor one, let us consider what it means, in the most basic methodological sense, to gear our efforts to working up a model on, say, the role of the Soviet military. Assume that one was capable of elucidating in quite convincing fashion an array of characteristics of the relationship between the Soviet military and the political leadership that overall showed the military to be: (1) because of its peculiar values, basically out of step with the political leadership in attaching overriding importance to such things as high defense spending, professional autonomy, and so on; and (2) because of its intrinsic institutional significance and basic cohesion, apparently capable of influencing decisions from time to time in accord with those values. This, to be sure, is but a sketch of the main elements that might go to make up a relatively sophisticated looking model of Soviet civil-military relations.

But where does one go from here? To what extent can that

model be relied upon to have a genuine explanatory (much less predictive) utility in cases of concern to the policymaker? While such a model might seem convincing as the basic characterization of Soviet civil-military relations, when juxtaposed, say, to a contrary model, essentially in the abstract, it cannot be assumed that the particular case at issue would fit the general pattern. It may be an exception—even a quite rare exception—that would not conform to one or more of the basic premises of the model. It may not involve the differences in political and military values assumed in the model; the military's intrinsic institutional significance may not apply; and, indeed, it may be an issue in which it makes no sense to talk about the military as a whole at all.

The point here is simply that a model (particularly one that purports to encompass such a large phenomenon as Soviet civil military relations) should reasonably be expected to provide a fair amount of guidance as to when and where it is most and least likely to apply. This calls for great and genuine sophistication, which implies in turn much data-gathering and testing. In the case of the model sketched above, for example, one would want at minimum such refinements as a delineation of the kinds of circumstances in which particular military and political values would be more or less out of phase, the kinds of circumstances in which the military's institutional significance would matter, and the kinds of circumstances in which the military would be more or less *the* military.[13]

Lacking such refinements, one is left with an analytic device of great pretension but dubious utility. Indeed, perhaps the most fundamental disutility is that not only will such a model interpret exceptional cases wrongly, but it will by its very assumptions impede recognition in the first place of what is exceptional. This, of course, will delay timely resort to some more viable analytic alternative.

None of this is intended to impose impossibly high

standards on efforts to apply basic social science techniques in the Soviet setting. Even under the best of analytical circumstances, operating within the confines of a particular model—no matter how encompassing and elaborate it may be—is bound to make the recognition of exceptional cases somewhat difficult.[14] Hence, one is always well advised to keep an open mind about going outside a particular model to seek the corrective aid of alternative analytic constructs.[15] Moreover, it is appreciated that to some extent it is putting the cart before the horse to expect a model to have in its early adumbration the attributes it may be able to acquire only after extensive use and testing.

However, this is the very nub of the matter with respect to the impact a focus on model building can make on our appreciation of the data problems involved in fathoming Soviet strategic arms decisions. After all, we are in significant ways prisoners of the very words we use, the very terms we adopt to describe things. There is a certain aesthetic appeal that beckons one to construct elaborate analytical devices of one's own. There is a certain appearance of respectability that urges one to be in fashion as an analyst. There is a certain satisfaction that comes with the feeling that one's intellectual labors are responsive to the big policy questions of the day. Unfortunately, these can combine to make us think and talk and write as if we had in hand, or could find just around the corner, models that deal with such big topics as the role of the Soviet military and hold out to the policymaker real promise. But, by any reasonably strict standards, aren't we only really capable of dealing at present in rather crude hypotheses about some aspects of civil-military relations in the USSR with but limited (and certainly not reliably predictive) utility for the policymaker?

Lowering our sights to perceive more clearly what is involved when one seeks to acquire knowledge in the social sciences may help our efforts to be judged more realistically and to be ultimately more responsive to the needs of the policymaker. Otherwise, expectations will be raised that cannot possibly be fulfilled and in that failure the myth may be encouraged (or perhaps perpetuated) that assessing such matters as Soviet strategic arms programs is mostly a physical science problem anyway and that where social science judgments do apply, vehemence and repetition are as good standards as any.

The present study has tried to take its cue from the very basic notion that what may be the most important aspect of Soviet life to get answers about is also that aspect of Soviet life about which the Soviets are most secretive. This means on the face of it that in this setting the scholar's temptation to rush to judgment must be particularly tempered by an appreciation that bad answers could be dangerous answers and that bad answers are easy to come by. The study has also tried to take its cue from something more basic than particular models or analytic constructs themselves. How can we get to the point where we can usefully generalize about something? Do we basically repeat (in perhaps ever fancier language) our original surmise until we have convinced ourselves and others that we must be correct? Or do we rather try as best we can to keep reminding ourselves that we are dealing only with a surmise until we have accumulated as much evidence as we possibly can to support it and tested it against other surmises?

In a sense, all scholarship is a kind of Thomistic enterprise where faith and reason—and faith in reason—are brought together. It takes faith in our original hypothesis about something to be willing to undertake the difficult business of trying to demonstrate that reason supports it. But it takes faith in reason to be willing to reject that hypothesis if reason does not support it. In the case of St. Thomas Aquinas himself, it would perhaps have been too much to expect that an atheistic outcome could have been a real possibility. In our case, however, in pursuing the Thomistic enterprise in trying to understand Soviet strategic arms decisions, there should at least be room for genuine agnosticism. After all, if we are to be taken seriously in dealing with such matters, we should be prepared to acknowledge that, on more than one occasion, the most respectable and responsible answer we can offer may be a simple and straightforward "I don't know."

8
A Multiple Approach Analysis of the SS-6 Program

The application of multiple-approach analyses to Soviet strategic arms decisions is likely to be a large and difficult task. Nevertheless, it is neither so formidable nor lacking in importance to remain unattempted. What follows is an illustration of how one might at least begin to examine the decisions on the first Soviet ICBM.

Background

The SS-6 program has been selected for analysis because of its intrinsic significance and its value for illustrative purposes. As the initial Soviet ICBM, the SS-6 was an important step in the evolution of the Soviet-U.S. strategic arms relationship. Moreover, it is still a controversial program from the standpoint of Western analysis.[1]

It was expected by many in the late 1950s, after the SS-6 made its international debut (first in a successful Soviet test in August 1957 and then as the launcher of sputnik in October of that year), that the Soviets would seek to produce and deploy the system in large numbers, which led in turn to fears that the United States might confront a missile gap in the early 1960s. Yet the gap that eventually materialized favored the United States. The Soviets had in fact deployed only a "handful" of their first-generation ICBMs.[2] And according to many interpretations, they subsequently sought to create proxy ICBMs to close the gap by emplacing medium-range ballistic missiles (MRBMs) and intermediate-range ballistic missiles (IRBMs) in Cuba—thus precipitating the Cuban missile crisis in October 1962.

In addition to its intrinsic significance, the SS-6 program is useful as an illustrative multiple-approach case study. The program can, by no means, be probed in detail here. An appropriate "testing" of approaches would require extensive analysis and the probable use of classified materials. However, a survey of various elements of, and circumstances surrounding, the SS-6 program suggests that it may be particularly amenable to analysis along the lines of the three approaches examined in this study.

In using multiple-approach analysis, as was suggested in the introduction to this study, one approach may be more persuasive than others in explaining particular kinds of Soviet strategic arms decisions. It may well be found, for example, that strategic calculation was the dominant factor in determining some decision. In another, pluralistic pressure may emerge with relatively more weight. In yet another, national leadership preferences may carry the argument. In short, because of data constraints or the particular nature of the strategic arms decision in question, certain approaches are simply likely to be more fruitful and persuasive than others. But we can justifiably arrive at this conclusion only after we have given a number of approaches a fair trial in examining a particular decision-making case.

This treatment of the SS-6 program cannot offer anything approaching a firm conclusion as to whether all or any of the analytic approaches treated are valid in this instance. It is only intended to help make the case for using multiple approaches by indicating the kinds of questions that are likely to be ignored or slighted if one does not do so. Those questions may ultimately be important to a satisfactory explanation of the decisions in this controversial program.

The Contribution of a Rational Strategic Actor Perspective

Given its emphasis on the import of strategic calculation in the deliberations of Soviet decision makers, a rational strategic actor approach seems particularly appropriate in examining the SS-6 program. Whatever the value of the other approaches in shedding light on the program, it would be a mistake to slight the sorts of considerations to which this approach directs one's attention. As indicated in the discussion in Part 1, this approach requires the analyst (1) to emphasize strategic calculation, in the military sense of the word, in order to gauge the strategic "weight" of the decision; (2) to take into account pertinent strategic values that might be peculiarly Soviet; and (3) to indicate how a rational strategic actor decision could plausibly be taken in the Soviet defense decision-making environment.

Strategic Weight of the SS-6 Decisions

With respect to the first task, it should be noted that the strategic value of the program can be viewed in the broad sense of the term. Indeed, the best extant rational actor interpretation of the SS-6 program focuses on the importance to the Soviets of its political utility, particularly in pursuit of Soviet foreign policy objectives in Berlin in the late 1950s and early 1960s.[3] And it is argued in this interpretation that it was this broader foreign policy concern that in fact prompted the Soviets (and particularly Khrushchev) to persist in publicly making claims about the pace and success of the program that later turned out to be gross exaggerations. As earlier suggested, it is possible that this broader "strategic" dimension of the SS-6 program could best be evaluated along national leadership decision-making lines, whereby attention is pointedly drawn to policy inputs by top decision makers that would extend beyond strategic calculation in the strict military sense. But in any event, this politico-strategic dimension should not be overlooked in evaluating the SS-6 decisions.

The primary question the rational strategic actor approach should pose concerns the military value of the SS-6 effort to the Soviets. In the strategic context of the late 1950s, the development, production, and deployment of the SS-6 would seem a rational course for the Soviets to have taken. Since the SS-6 was the first Soviet ICBM, the decisions on it would probably have had considerable strategic weight. The program could well have been regarded as something of considerable value from the standpoint of the strategic balance between the United States and the Soviet Union. Presumably, an assumption along these lines underlay the belief in the West at the time that the Soviets were intent on creating a missile gap in their advantage; hence, Khrushchev's public claims with regard to the program seemed quite credible.[4]

Ironically, the strategic weight of the SS-6 decisions seems all the greater in view of the failure of the Soviets to create a bomber gap as had been predicted in the West but a few years earlier. It is quite plausible (and probably seemed so to Western analysts in the late 1950s) that a key reason why the Soviets did not push ahead with strategic bombers was that they planned to improve their strategic standing vis-à-vis the United States with ICBMs instead. In short, when the SS-6 program is viewed in rational strategic actor terms, with a focus on the military value of the decisions, a determined Soviet ICBM effort seems eminently reasonable.

Soviet Military Values

As noted, inherent in the rational strategic actor approach is a focus on peculiar Soviet military values. In other words, while it would seem to have made good sense on the basis of U.S. strategic rationality for the Soviets to have pushed ahead quickly with their first ICBM program, did it make equally good sense from a *Soviet* point of view? For the present, the general question can only be posed here; an assessment of Soviet strategic values with regard to the significance and utility of ICBMs would have to be made on the basis of an extensive evaluation of doctrine and practices, a sorting out of particular service biases, and the like. It would seem, for example, on the face of it, that the Soviet artillery emphasis over the years would have been congenial to a subsequent rocket stress when the SS-6 was in the offing. Yet, in his memoirs, Khrushchev makes a point of singling out Soviet artillerymen as opponents of missiles.[5]

Peculiar Soviet military values that should not be overlooked are those that pertain to command and control considerations in particular. It is tempting to view technical shortcomings in the SS-6 as the key obstacle impeding the Soviets from taking the apparent rational strategic course of pushing ahead with their first ICBM program. Indeed, in that event the rational course would have been to wait on, and then push ahead with, a presumably better second-generation ICBM.[6] Khrushchev, for example, notes in his memoirs that the SS-6, designed by Korolyov, could not "be fired at a moments notice" and that another designer, Yangel, "tackled the problem of perfecting a rocket that could be launched on short notice."[7] According to a Western analysis, the SS-6's deficiency in this regard was due to "its reliance on nonstorable cryogenic fuels . . . (which) makes launching it a long and awkward process during which it is especially vulnerable in conditions of war."[8]

It is not to deny the essential accuracy of these evaluations, however, to suggest that the significance of these shortcomings of the SS-6 would have depended in part on Soviet command and control perspectives with respect to ICBMs.[9] As implied by Khrushchev, the Soviets were eager for a quick-reaction capability, which in turn implies a certain willingness to live with the risks (for example, of accidental war if control should fail) of maintaining ICBMs in a high-readiness posture. Yet, as one Western analyst has noted, "Soviet strategic forces never went on alert, even during the Cuban missile crisis, until the mid-to-late sixties."[10] If this statement is correct, the Soviets evidenced a command and control conservatism that was not readily consistent with placing a premium on being able to launch "on short notice,"even after they presumably acquired ICBMs in the 1960s that remedied the deficiencies of the SS-6. None of this means, of course, that the Soviets regarded the technical shortcomings of the SS-6 lightly. It only means that from the Soviet perspective those shortcomings on their own may not have been a compelling reason for deciding to deploy only a small number of first-generation ICBMs. Thus, while it is important to take the technical shortcomings of the SS-6 into account, it is also necessary to look at other factors that may have influenced the decisions on the program.[11]

Decision-making Practices

As suggested earlier, by and large, interpretations that have been more or less based on rational actor assumptions have not devoted explicit attention to decision making. That focus has been adopted by interpretations challenging the rational actor view. It is important, however, to meet those challenges on their own ground, particularly so in analyzing Soviet strategic arms decisions. There are, as we have noted, particular arrangements and practices in the Soviet defense decision-making setting that would seem to make rational strategic actor behavior possible and also shape that behavior in significant ways. It is only possible here, however, to note the salience of one of the key features of this environment: mid-term defense planning.

It is notable that in August 1957 the SS-6 was first successfully tested [12] and that in September it was announced that the sixth five-year economic plan was to be cut short. Preparation commenced for launching a new seven-year plan, which was formally adopted at the Twenty-first Party Congress in February 1959.[13] Whether the broader economic implications of decisions on the SS-6 program prompted the leadership's moves with respect to overall economic planning scarcely a month after the August test is difficult to say. However, it seems reasonably likely in any event that, except for earlier development decisions, there would have been significant consideration of the production and eventual deployment of the first-generation ICBM in the period when the new seven-year plan was being debated.[14]

As has been suggested, decisions that occur in the period of defense plan preparation, which presumably coincides with overall economic plan preparation, would seem to be the likeliest to reflect the impact of the international action-reaction phenomenon. And the rational strategic actor approach would appear most sensitive to the operation of that phenomenon. Whether the SS-6 program in fact registered this impact cannot be ventured here. The point, however, is to emphasize that the rational strategic actor approach would clearly seem to have some value in calling attention to that possibility—not only by calling attention to the strategic weight of the SS-6 program (and the likelihood that the program, unlike some others, would have mandated extensive top-level scrutiny), but also in pointing up the relevance of mid-term defense planning.[15]

If, indeed, certain key decisions on the SS-6 were taken at the time that priorities were being debated for the next overall mid-term economic plan, nonmilitary considerations may also have come into play. Since the Soviets did not adopt what would seem (at least at the time) to have been the rational strategic course by pushing the SS-6 program vigorously, and since from a Soviet command and control perspective, at least, the technical deficiencies may not have been regarded as a sufficient reason not to do so, nonmilitary considerations seem quite important. But first, other "military" considerations should be taken into account.

The Contribution of a Pluralistic Perspective

As noted in the discussion of the pluralistic decision-making approach in Part 1, there is a temptation to turn to this approach to explain Soviet decisions that appear aberrant or "irrational" from a U.S. strategic perspective. The possibility should not be ruled out, however, that pluralistic pressures can also eventuate in a "rational" decision (according to U.S. or Soviet strategic values), for example, as a consequence of some sort of equilibrium being established among competing selfish interests in a particular weapon program.[16] Nevertheless, in the SS-6 case, the temptation to rely on the pluralistic approach is strong, precisely because the Soviets avoided what appears to have been the rational strategic course of action by eventually deploying the system only in minuscule numbers. On the other hand, one might well argue that as a system with considerable potential strategic weight, extensive top-level scrutiny of the SS-6 program would have occurred and would have acted to override or forestall the impact of pluralistic pressures. A decision (or set of decisions) on a program with only marginal strategic weight might more likely reflect the shaping influence of parochial pressures. Unless extensive top-level deliberation of all weapon systems is possible, the scrutiny may be only perfunctory for some weapon programs, thus permitting pluralistically shaped programs to slip through as line-item entries.

These considerations notwithstanding, the apparent failure of the rational strategic actor approach to explain the decision(s) taken suggests that the SS-6 program should be examined along pluralistic decision-making lines also. More particularly, the very nature of the weapon system in question suggests the applicability of a pluralistic decision-making analysis. The SS-6 program is representative of those defense decisions that are likely to have a substantial unsettling effect on various organizational and personal relationships within the defense establishment. Anticipation of considerable gains or fear of considerable loss of resources, prestige, and the like would probably stimulate interest-group activity. As the first Soviet ICBM, the SS-6 weapon system called into question established service roles and missions. It seems reasonable to expect therefore that certain decisions (affecting at least its production and deployment) were not removed from the pulling and hauling that presumably took place over the establishment of a new service arm—the Strategic Rocket Forces (SRF)—by late 1959.[17]

Service Interests

Graham Allison has offered a pluralistic explanation of the limited SS-6 deployment by focusing on the service interests connected with the Soviet MRBM effort. His basic case rests on two points. First, since the SRF had not yet been set up, there was no strong organizational proponent for the ICBM. Second, since Soviet MRBMs were under the jurisidiction of an existing service arm, MRBMs (and incipient IRBMs) were pushed to the detriment of the ICBM effort.[18] The result was the extensive deployment of M/IRBMs by the early 1960s, "three times European overkill," and the deployment of only a "handful" of SS-6s.

On its face, Allison's argument seems quite plausible. By itself, however, it neither tells the whole story, in terms of the kinds of considerations to which the other approaches might draw our attention, nor takes into account other pluralistic interests that would appear to be pertinent. As to the first, the strength of the arguments by M/IRBM proponents would seem to have depended heavily on the Soviets' evaluation of the strategic weight of the SS-6 program and their estimate of the significance of its technical problems—considerations that a rational strategic actor perspective helps to highlight. Moreover, an estimate of the role of the service pressures involved should also take into account designer interests and defense-industrial interests.[19] These other interests would seem quite relevant to an examination of the SS-6 program, and when they are entered into the pluralistic equation, a sturdy alliance on behalf of the M/IRBM effort (to the detriment of the SS-6) may not automatically be supported.

Designer Interests

As mentioned above, Khrushchev identified Korolyov as the designer of the SS-6 and Yangel as the designer of the successor ICBM which, in Khrushchev's view, overcame the deficiencies of the SS-6.[20] Khrushchev further noted: "Yangel also worked on medium-range ballistic missiles that could travel 2,000 to 4,000 kilometers."[21] Western analysts have called attention to the competition between designers in the Soviet defense establishment in general,[22] and, given the aforementioned missile responsibilities, such competition between Yangel and Korolyov would seem to have been quite natural. However, in a study of Korolyov's role in the Soviet space program, a somewhat different view is given of their relationship, at least in the early 1950s. "Yangel . . . made every effort to work along with Korolyov. But Chalomei put up a determined opposition to their collaboration, with the result that the two men never worked together in the full sense."[23]

The accuracy of this description of the relationship between Korolyov and Yangel either in the early 1950s or later on when the designers were thrust into apparent competitive roles cannot be evaluated here. However, it would seem prudent to take this description into account in examining their respective incentives to push particular missile efforts. Moreover, while it would seem reasonable to equate Yangel's MRBM interest with that of the service branch pushing MRBMs, caution should be exercised. Although Yangel (as the designer of both MRBMs and ICBMs) would have presumably been some sort of competitor of Korolyov, where did his priorities lie?

If Yangel's major concern was the MRBMs, he would appear a natural ally of the traditional service arm with MRBM jurisdiction. However, if his major concern was with promoting an improved ICBM to supersede Korolyov's SS-6, his interests may well have diverged from those of that service, which presumably viewed ICBM's in general as a challenge to its established roles and missions. On the other side of the coin, Korolyov's incentive to push the SS-6 as an ICBM may not have been as strong as one would at first tend to assume. Despite the fact that the SS-6 was eventually deployed only in minuscule numbers as the first Soviet ICBM, it was used extensively in the late 1950s and in the 1960s as the workhorse of the Soviet space program.[24] Korolyov's concern to promote the SS-6 as an ICBM may thus have been considerably attenuated by its bright prospects in the space program.

Defense-Industrial Interests

In addition to the interests of key Soviet weapon designers, the interests of other important members of the defense-industrial establishment must be taken into account.[25] It is not clear on the basis of available materials just what the ministerial jurisdiction of Soviet missile efforts in the late 1950s might have been. But it is known, for example, that ballistic missile programs have been basically the responsibility of the Ministry of General Machinebuilding since its establishment in 1965.[26] The missile efforts of the late 1950s and early 1960s, therefore, must have been conducted under the aegis of one or more of the existing defense-industrial ministries. Khrushchev notes that, with respect to missiles, "we started turning them out like sausages at our aircraft plants."[27] This suggests that at least some missile efforts at the time may have been under the authority of the Ministry of the Aviation Industry.[28]

Although there are few details to go on, various organizational considerations could hold important implications for an assessment of defense-industrial interests in the SS-6 program. First of all, it is curious, to say the least, that the Soviets established a service arm (the SRF) in late 1959 to accommodate the ICBM, yet waited almost six years to reflect the advent of this new weapon system in the organizational arrangements in the defense-industrial sector. Surely there was some justification for a new ministry devoted primarily to ballistic missiles by the early 1960s at least, when Khrushchev was making the SRF the premier service and when, especially after the Cuban missile crisis, a Soviet missile buildup seemed in order.

Against this backdrop, the tardiness in establishing the Ministry of General Machinebuilding suggests that resistance on the part of existing defense-industrial ministries may have been encountered. The new ministry undoubtedly was not created out of whole cloth. For example, it must have taken missile resources away from the ministry (or ministries) originally charged with that production responsibility. Moreover if, as suggested above, the establishment of the SRF, and the subsequent primacy accorded it by Khrushchev, ruffled the feathers of the other services, that too may have had an impact. Would it have made sense for Khrushchev to have antagonized both the services and the defense-industrial ministries at the same time? What these considerations might mean for an assessment of the SS-6 program is by no means clear. But that a pluralistic assessment of the program that excludes these considerations is deficient seems evident enough.

To speculate briefly in this regard, the SS-6 program may have stimulated a number of contrary concerns. For example, assuming an interest on the part of the existing defense-industrial ministry (or ministries) in retaining missile production responsibility, once it was secured, one could argue that the ministry with jurisdiction over the SS-6 would have been likely to push the SS-6 program. If, as Khrushchev hints, the Ministry of the Aviation Industry held this jurisdiction, a sizable SS-6 production effort could have been an attractive means of compensating for the failure of a large intercontinental bomber program to materialize (which belied the earlier Western bomber gap estimates). On the other side of the coin, the ministry presumably had already been compensated for this failure to some considerable extent by the authorization of a large medium-range bomber program. Roughly 1,100 of those bombers (the Badger) had been produced and gone into operation by mid-1959.[29] (And a follow-on medium bomber, the Blinder, was under development.[30]) The ministry's enthusiasm for pushing the SS-6 program may also have been tempered by the consideration that a large ICBM effort might call more quickly to the Soviet political leadership's attention the need for a separate ministry to conduct the Soviet ballistic missile effort.

There are additional complicating considerations that might be taken into account. Since Khrushchev's remark on the production of missiles in aircraft plants is the only substantial hint of the Ministry of the Aviation Industry's jurisdiction in the Soviet missile effort in the late 1950s, it is not clear whether the SS-6 program was in fact under that ministry, or whether the MRBM effort and Yangel's successor ICBM program were also under it. But an assessment of defense-industrial interests requires consideration of jurisdictional relationships nonetheless.

If, for example, Yangel's MRBM program was under one ministry and Korolyov's ICBM program under another, one could argue that the respective ministries might have backed their resident missile designers. But even here, in light of the various distinctions noted earlier, a tidy congruence of designer and ministry interests cannot be merely assumed (much less an entente involving service elements as well). The picture could also change if the MRBM effort and Korolyov's SS-6 program were under the same ministry. Presumably the interests of the ministry and its top officials would have been best served if both MRBMs and ICBMs were vigorously pushed. But if a choice had to be made (as seems to have been the case), it is difficult to say which of the missile efforts the ministry might have decided to back. At the very least, on these grounds alone, the ministry's interest in either would seem less than that of the designers involved.

It also should be noted that the defense-industrial ministries were not really ministries for most of this time. They were affected by the extensive economic reorganization that was instituted in the spring of 1957, which created regional economic councils (*sovnarkhozy*) and eliminated or weakened the central economic ministries. Originally, perhaps, as the need for this reform was being debated, there may have been some thought of doing away with the defense-industrial ministries and transferring their responsibilities to the regional economic councils.[31] But when the reform went into effect, the defense-industrial ministries seemed to be excepted.

In December 1957, however, the defense-industrial ministries (with one exception) were "transformed" into state committees.[32] It is easy to overstate the significance of name changes in analyzing the Soviet bureaucracy, but in this instance the name change may well have signified real organizational rearrangements. Two of the state committees had the term technology added to their title: the State Committee for Aviation Technology and the State Committee for Defense Technology. This suggests that the defense-industrial ministries, or at least those two ministries, may have been given a mandate to focus on research and development and that some (or all) of their production responsibilities went to regional economic councils.[33]

With respect to the SS-6 program, the effects of the economic reorganization may have been significant. The Soviet missile effort as a whole may have been regarded as too important (and already burdened with enough other uncertainties, technical and otherwise) to be impinged upon directly by these broader organizational considerations. Yet it cannot be ruled out that the perspectives of the relevant defense-industrial ministries (or, strictly speaking, after December 1957, state committees) on the program were affected nonetheless. If, for example, these ministries came to see their primary concern as defense technology, then the question of perfecting Yangel's successor system to the SS-6, rather than pushing ahead with SS-6 production, takes on a new dimension. In short, there may have been stronger interest from ministry types in the successor system because it was in the research and development stage and relatively weaker interest in the production fate of the SS-6.

Basic Significance of Pluralistic Decision Making

None of the considerations as presented here on service, designer, and defense-industrial interests should be regarded as more than that—considerations. After extensive examination, it may be found that very few of these considerations really mattered in shaping the SS-6 program. But a pluralistic approach to the SS-6 decisions requires that these (and likely other) considerations be taken into account.

One cannot focus on service or designer or defense-industrial interests alone to make a satisfactory pluralistic examination of the SS-6 case. The strength of the interests that were brought to bear (if they were) and the chance that those interests really mattered would seem to depend critically on the interrelationships of all the pertinent interested parties. Service, designer, and defense-industrial pressures could have coalesced to make a powerful case—for example, against heavy SS-6 production and deployment. But on the other hand, they could have cancelled each other out. We have no way of making a reasonable estimate on this score, however, if we do not take all of the interests into account and subject them to extensive analysis.

Just as the pluralistic approach cannot yield fruitful answers if one's focus is narrow within the confines of this approach, so too what the approach can tell us depends on considerations that it does not readily call attention to. As noted above, the strength of pluralistic pressures in the SS-6 case would seem to depend in the first instance on the strategic weight of the SS-6 system in the estimate of the top Soviet decision makers and their appreciation of the ramifications of the system's technical shortcomings. (Alternatively, the explanatory utility of these rational strategic actor considerations cannot really be gauged without taking pluralistic factors into account.) Similarly, the significance of pluralistic pressures would also seem to depend on considerations that the national leadership approach highlights. Did the Soviet leaders have personal preferences in defense or civilian matters in the late 1950s, when the SS-6 decisions were taken, that would have conflicted with or supported the various interests at work in the Soviet defense establishment? Did Khrushchev in particular have personal concerns that would have shaped the SS-6 decisions in a way that neither strategic calculation nor pluralistic pressures would explain?

The Contribution of a National Leadership Perspective

Placing rational strategic actor and pluralistic decision-making assumptions in realistic perspective in the Soviet environment requires paying heed to a middle ground those approaches tend to slight. This means focusing on the Soviet leaders, not just as strategic calculators, not just as individuals who might succumb to constituent pressures, but as leaders who have a country to run, as well as defense policies to pursue, and who therefore may have particular preferences with regard to economic, political, and other concerns that could impact on their judgments on defense decisions. The use of the national leadership perspective is especially commended to help explain the SS-6 decisions on the grounds that the personal concerns of the principal

Soviet leader, Khrushchev, seem to be quite visible in this period; those concerns could have affected his judgment on the SS-6.

Khrushchev's Standing in the Late 1950s

By way of offering a very rough balance sheet on the Soviet leadership situation in the period under consideration, it might be ventured that Khrushchev had probably pretty much passed through the period of maximum political jockeying in his political career, when he would seem to have been most susceptible to pressures from below. And this, it should be stressed, is important to take into account in assessing whether pluralistic pressures or leadership preferences may have had more weight in shaping the SS-6 program. Khrushchev had basically subdued his principal political rivals by this time (late 1957) by frustrating the efforts of the "anti-party group" to unseat him in June 1957. And by October 1957—one month into the preparations for the seven-year plan—he had presumably tightened his hold on the military establishment by ousting Marshal Zhukov as minister of defense.

Before examining Khrushchev's personal concerns, it is useful to underscore the point that the prefrences of other Soviet leaders should not be ignored, and indeed Khrushchev himself may not have done so. Michel Tatu offers the following cautionary perspective on Khrushchev's standing:

> Khrushchev had indeed won a brilliant victory in June 1957 over a coalition of his main political adversaries, but the abscess was very slow in draining. It took the whole of 1958 to eliminate Bulganin, who lost the chairmanship of the Council of Ministers in March, his membership in the Party Presidium in September, and was officially implicated in the "anti-party group" only in November. Two other members of the "group," Pervukhin and Saburov, were implicated only at the Twenty-first Congress in January 1959, and even then, as in June 1957, Pervukhin kept his seat as alternate

member to the Presidium and Saburov kept his Central
Committee membership. The last of the "anti-party"
men, Marshal Voroshilov, was still chief of state and member
of the Presidium. Not until the Twenty-second Congress in
October 1961 was he accused and forced to confess.[34]

Pervukhin and Saburov presumably had some personal
preferences, at least with respect to defense matters, since
they had both been defense-industrial ministers in the early
1950s.[35] Similarly, to name but one other leader, Frol Kozlov
(who was not implicated in the anti-party group maneuver),
whose star was on the rise in the late 1950s and who emerged
as Khrushchev's putative heir in the early 1960s ("heir," that
is, by dint of his apparent role as leader of the opposition to
Khrushchev subsequent to the political demise of the key
figures in the anti-party group), also can be presumed to
have had particular defense concerns. D.F. Ustinov, the
principal defense sector overseer, was affiliated with him.[36]
And it is especially noteworthy that S.A. Afanasyev, who
became minister of the ballistic missile Ministry of General
Machinebuilding in 1965, had career connections to Kozlov.
Kozlov's political power base was in the Leningrad party
organization, and from 1958 to 1961, Afanasyev was chairman of the Leningrad Regional Economic Council.[37]
This latter connection suggests an intriguing line of
inquiry. It is prudent to avoid assuming that the "pork
barrel" phenomenon, which might shape defense programs
to some degree in the United States (for example, with
respect to bases, installations, and the like being established
in certain congressional districts), would similarly obtain in
the Soviet Union. Soviet leaders, after all, are not known for
their responsiveness to the electorate at large. Nevertheless, if
there was ever a time in the postwar era when the phenomenon might have operated, it was in the late 1950s when the
regional party secretaries had particular political clout and
when they were, in effect, in charge of the regional economic
councils in their respective areas of jurisdiction. One can

only speculate at this point that, given the defense production responsibilities that certain of these economic councils might have had, regional economic concerns expressed by local party leaders (and certain top leaders as well) may have impinged on Soviet defense decisions— including those related to the SS-6.

In any event, what should be stressed at present is simply that Khrushchev's personal preferences probably mattered most in shaping the SS-6 decisions, but that the preferences of other Soviet leaders may have mattered to some degree as well. Without extensive investigation, however, it is impossible to know whether they did, whether constituent pressure rather than personal preference affected the views of individual leaders, and whether, by dint of pressure or preference, those individuals would have pushed the SS-6 program or opposed it on behalf of other military or civilian concerns.[38]

Khrushchev's Space Program Concerns

As noted in our discussion of Korolyov's incentives to lobby for the SS-6 in the late 1950s, the SS-6 became the workhorse of the Soviet space program. In light of the intensity of the Soviet space effort in the late 1950s and early 1960s, the "handful" of SS-6s eventually deployed as ICBMs is by no means an accurate reflection of the overall production program for the SS-6. Some sixteen successful Soviet space shots took place by 1962, according to one reckoning.[39] Failures also must be taken into account, as well as production for test purposes. If therefore the Soviets had elected to forego or mount only a modest space effort, more than a "handful" of SS-6s could have been deployed as ICBMs, assuming of course that in the absence of the space effort the Soviets would have been so inclined.

Even a cursory look at the situation suggests that the Soviets (and particularly Khrushchev) regarded a vigorous space effort as important. Leonid Vladimirov's account of the Soviet space effort suggests, for example, that Korolyov informed the political leaders that the Soviet Union would have the capability, in the form of his SS-6, to launch the first earth satellite in the International Geophysical Year (mid-1957 to mid-1958). According to Vladimirov, Korolyov was stimulated to make this claim by articles in the American scientific press advocating a similar course of action for the United States. The go-ahead was given and a crash effort resulted in the sputnik launching in October 1957.

Vladimirov maintains that Khrushchev's interest was particularly sparked by the chance to "overtake America" in at least this field.[40] Subsequently, the competitive urge shifted to putting the first man into space. In this respect, Korolyov "kept on persuading the Party leaders—in effect, Khrushchev—to put more and more factories, design offices and research laboratories at his disposal . . . . by skillfully exploiting his first successes he succeeded in obtaining a great deal."[41]

Although the accuracy of his account cannot be properly gauged here, Vladimirov would seem to offer reasonable evidence of Khrushchev's personal concern with the Soviet space program, especially when considered against the backdrop of two fairly firm facts: (1) whatever he was at the time, that is, from the summer of 1957 on, Khrushchev was at least first among equals in the political leadership; and (2) the Soviets did mount a vigorous space effort at the time. In this context, there are certain considerations that should be probed in some detail. To what extent, for example, was Khrushchev pressured by Korolyov to support a large space effort? While it is impossible to assess the significance of Korolyov's lobbying, it would seem likely that much would have depended on Khrushchev's personal preferences. For one thing, the attribution of considerable clout to Korolyov in this case is not readily consistent with his apparent lack of clout in pushing the SS-6 as an ICBM. (Although, as noted, the space program option may have weakened his incentive to push the SS-6 as an ICBM.) Moreover, the urge to beat the United States in space was quite consistent with Khrushchev's oft-touted remarks about overtaking the United States in a broad variety of fields.[42]

Indeed, Khrushchev did not seem unaware of the implications of Soviet space triumphs in at least the broader strategic sense. As he put it, in his memoirs, "Eventually, we began to launch our Sputniks, which made our potential enemies cringe in fright but made many other people glow with joy."[43] And this was a period, it might also be recalled, when the Soviets (and particularly Khrushchev) were busy courting the Third World, trying to sell the Soviet model of development as a better model than the Western one—hence making Soviet space successes a particularly valuable symbol of the Soviet system as the wave of the future.

In short, for the Soviets and Khrushchev personally, the space effort was a serious business deserving of priority treatment. Obviously, the strategic relationship with the United States in the strict military sense was hardly a trivial concern. But is seems impossible to rule out the impingement of Khrushchev's space program concerns on his judgment regarding the SS-6 program. It is conceivable that he would have preferred both a vigorous space effort and a large deployment of ICBMs. But if it was necessary to make some compromise, how important would his space concerns have been? The weight of these concerns should be gauged by taking into account other preferences Khrushchev may have had as a national leader, as well as the considerations to which the other analytical perspectives call attention.

Khrushchev's Agricultural Concerns

Khrushchev's personal interest in agricultural matters was a hallmark of his career. During his rise in the 1950s, after Stalin's death, the success of his famous and risky virgin lands program in the first few years after its inauguration (in

1954) probably contributed significantly to his political fortunes. There is evidence that his interest in agriculture did not wane subsequently and that it was an important concern in the period of deliberation on the seven-year plan—when decisions on the production and eventual deployment of the SS-6 would have been considered.

Questions of securing appropriate levels of agricultural equipment were raised in the plan preparation period. It is not within the purview of this study to try to correlate the ups and downs of agricultural investment with even apparent defense spending shifts. But agricultural mechanization was a topic of deep concern to the Soviets (and particularly Khrushchev) in the overall context in which SS-6 production and deployment were probably considered, and Khrushchev may have viewed the SS-6 program and the agricultural mechanization effort as being, in some sense, competing economic priorities.

As one indicator of the concern with agricultural mechanization, it is noteworthy that between 1953 and 1961, 1957 was the peak year for production of agricultural machinery.[44] Since the decisions for this production would not have fallen within the preparation period for the seven-year plan (September 1957 to February 1959), they of course cannot be taken to conflict with decisions taken on the SS-6 in this period. Yet the apparent emphasis given to the production of agricultural equipment in 1957 suggests that this production had come to be regarded as important by the time production and deployment decisions on the SS-6 were confronted in the plan preparation period. It is also noteworthy that agricultural equipment production fell off in 1958 and dropped even more in 1959.[45] What caused this downward trend is impossible to say without extensive analysis—and cannot be attributed directly to the gear-up for SS-6 production (whether as space launchers or ICBMs).

Another manifestation of concern with the problem of agricultural mechanization did occur in the 1957-59 plan preparation period, however. In January 1958, Khrushchev proposed the abolition of the Machine Tractor Stations (MTS), and a decree to that effect was promulgated in March of that year. Among other things, the apparent intent was to improve the utilization of existing agricultural equipment by placing the equipment under the direct control of collective farms.[46] A number of aspects of the MTS abolition are pertinent. First, even a cursory look suggests that the proposal was very much Khrushchev's personal initiative. Second, the nature of the move also suggests that Khrushchev was trying his best to solve the agricultural mechanization problem "on the cheap" by rationalizing the use of existing equipment to help take up the slack of needed equipment that was not produced. Third, the importance of the move to Khrushchev is indicated by the fact that he pushed it even though it did not go down easily. It was debated (and criticized) in the press. One account of the reaction to it suggests that the "professional" ideologists— particularly Presidium member (Politburo member) Mikhail Suslov[47]—regarded it as dangerous backsliding. What all of this seems to signify, so far as a limited investigation permits us to say, is that Khrushchev probably regarded agricultural mechanization as an important economic priority and that, in the period of preparation for the seven-year plan, he was looking for ways to somehow reconcile this priority with other priorities—possible space and defense needs.[48]

Since the tie-in between agricultural and defense needs cannot easily be made, it is useful to point up some indications from a later period that suggest that Khrushchev may well have viewed defense priorities and agricultural priorities in some conflict in the 1957-59 time frame. In January 1961, when Khrushchev was mounting a new push for increased agricultural machinery, he declared, "today our country . . . can, without jeopardizing the development of industry and the strengthening of its defense, devote more funds to the development of agriculture."[49] Following up this theme, two months later he noted, "leading officials . . . have erroneously concluded that the equipment now used in agriculture is fully adequate."[50]

In commenting on these remarks, Michel Tatu notes that Khrushchev's plans were frustrated at this time. And Tatu also takes note of a phenomenon by which, even after investments were already earmarked for agriculture, agricultural needs may have come into conflict with defense priorities.

> Whenever funds were unexpectedly needed in a sector of industry . . . the funds were always quietly but firmly abstracted from the poor relations of the Soviet economy. . . . In this way the appropriations for agriculture were unobtrusively cut several times during 1959 and 1960 . . . . All this was being done underhandedly, by "nibbling" as Khrushchev put it later.[51]

Where and how would this "nibbling" have taken place? As it stands, the above statement does not specifically tie agricultural equipment production and defense production together. Andrew Sheren has pointed out, however, that the Soviet defense industries also produce items for the civilian economy. And he further notes, "it is reasonable to suppose that MOP (Ministry of the Defense Industry) plants have the capacity to produce such items as tractors, agricultural equipment . . . etc."[52] In brief, it does not seem far-fetched to assume that if some appropriations for agriculture were unobtrusively shifted, it would have been most easy to do so wherever a joint responsibility was held for agricultural and other production. And defense-industrial ministries and possibly individual plants under their jurisdiction would seem to have had such a responsibility. (Nevertheless, it is recognized that in pursuing this kind of analysis one must be extremely careful to avoid assuming that agricultural production and defense production would naturally compete for the same resources at, say, the plant level. For the USSR, as for the United States, the problem of calculating the feasibility of resource transfers from defense to civilian uses, or vice versa, is huge and complex.)

None of this, to be sure, constitutes any firm tie-in between the SS-6 program and the production efforts for agricultural equipment in the late 1950s. Indeed, it is not at all clear from the foregoing considerations whether it was defense priorities or agricultural priorities that may have gotten short shrift in the late 1950s (or whether either of them really did). On the one hand, agricultural equipment production apparently did decline from the high level of 1957. But, on the other hand, the references to "unobtrusive" efforts to shift funds away from agriculture suggest that the allocations may still have been high enough to really detract from other programs—possibly defense programs. What seems reasonably clear at present is that Khrushchev had a strong personal concern for Soviet agricultural mechanization efforts and that there are grounds for believing that Khrushchev saw this concern as coming into conflict from time to time with defense efforts.[53]

Basic Significance of National Leadership Concerns

Overall, in calling attention to Khrushchev's space program and agricultural production concerns in the late 1950s, a national leadership approach would seem to have a contribution to make in explaining the SS-6 decisions. Extensive analysis along the lines of this approach would be necessary, however, to make any reasonable evaluation of the significance of these concerns, and also to determine if Khrushchev had other concerns that mattered or if the personal concerns of other Soviet leaders may have entered into the picture as well.[54]

For the present, it is sufficient to indicate that the national leadership approach calls attention to considerations that should be taken into account in assessing the SS-6 program—considerations that neither the rational strategic actor approach nor the pluralistic approach particularly encourages us to probe. Yet like those approaches, the national leadership perspective does not seem capable of standing on its own. As with the other approaches, the weight of the considerations the national leadership perspective emphasizes cannot be gauged in a vacuum. If, for example, we had no real feel for the Soviet estimate of the technical shortcomings of the SS-6, we might be led to overvalue the significance of Khrushchev's concerns for the space program or for agricultural equipment production in constraining the SS-6 program. Similarly, the significance we might attach to the technical shortcomings in impeding sizable deployment of the SS-6 could be quite different if we gave those national leadership considerations short shrift.

Implications

Although the task of fully analyzing the SS-6 decisions along multiple-approach lines basically remains to be done, the overview presented here suggests that each of the approaches examined in this study has an important, albeit partial, contribution to make to the effort. The use of each would seem to be supported by certain basic decision-making factors that are discernible in the setting in which decisions on the SS-6 probably took place. For example, the likelihood of high-level deliberation (in a mid-term economic plan preparation period) on a weapon system with apparently substantial strategic weight and significant performance drawbacks supports the use of the rational strategic actor approach. The likelihood of interest-group activity for or against a weapon system that challenged established service roles and missions and defense-industrial relationships supports use of the pluralistic approach. And finally, the likelihood of the impingement of leadership preferences, by a leader who had preferences that could have swayed his judgment on the SS-6 and who could have acted on the basis of those preferences without constituent pressure, supports use of the national leadership approach.

Equally important is that the SS-6 case helps to illustrate the point that, somewhat ironically, each approach may gain rather than simply lose plausibility by the simultaneous use of other approaches. This is more than a matter of a particular approach looking good by comparison. It is much easier, for example, to accept the possibility of tradeoffs involving service pulling and hauling or leadership concerns for agricultural equipment if one is also attentive to the kinds of considerations emphasized by the rational strategic actor approach—especially the technical shortcomings of the SS-6. It may be found that Khrushchev's agricultural equipment concerns might have carried sufficient weight to be the major impediment to the SS-6 program only because the SS-6 also had technical problems; alternatively, it may be found that the technical problems tipped the balance against sizable SS-6 deployment only because they emerged in a context in which the Soviet leader had other important concerns and priorities that the SS-6 program impinged upon. What matters for the present, however, is that as investigated thus far the SS-6 case suggests that by hewing to a single approach analysts may often be lulled into a false sense of security. They may not only be ignoring another line of analysis that is inherently more convincing (a risk one might understandably want to avoid), but in so doing they may also be depriving themselves of the kind of material it takes to make their own argument really convincing.

Just how far further analysis might take us in evaluating the SS-6 decisions cannot be hazarded at this point. Throughout the discussion, various considerations have been pointed up that might yield fruitful insights if pursued in more detail, particularly using classified information. But there is no way of knowing what such an investigation might reveal until it has actually been attempted.

In the meantime, the application of the three analytic approaches to the SS-6 decisions should not be regarded as establishing either directly or by default the validity of any one of the approaches.[55] The temptation to grant presumptive validity would appear to be greatest with respect to the rational strategic actor approach. The treatment of the other two approaches particularly shows, for example, how very complex an analysis of decision making in the SS-6 case can become. It suggests that, when all sources of information have been tapped, we may still be very far from what a pluralistic or national leadership approach (or some other decision-making approach) might be capable of revealing about a comparable U.S. strategic arms decision.

Consequently, since the pluralistic and national leadership approaches may seem to be much more in line with common notions about what constitutes decision-making analyses per se, the treatment of these approaches in the SS-6 might be taken to suggest that Soviet strategic arms decision-making analyses are bound to yield only speculation. By default, therefore, the rational strategic actor approach, which focuses on considerations (like strategy and weapons characteristics) that can be treated without reference to decision making and that, for the most part, have been so treated in analyses of Soviet strategic arms efforts over the years, can appear to stand on much firmer ground.

One might also be inclined to accord a presumptive validity to the rational strategic actor approach because the considerations it encompasses seem "harder" on their face. Compared with such inherently amorphous and soft phenomena as interests and preferences which one is compelled to emphasize in pursuing a pluralistic or national leadership analysis, the focus on strategic doctrine and weapons characteristics in the rational strategic actor approach is at least a focus on apparently much more tangible, and harder, analytic material.

Generally speaking, in certain major respects the difference is indeed real and significant for analysts trying to evaluate Soviet strategic arms efforts. With respect to Soviet strategic doctrine, the analyst can cite a tangible corpus of writings on some particular topic—such as the role of ICBMs—to make a case. And with regard to weapon characteristics, much of the data may be substantially harder than that with which the analyst has to deal in probing, say, leadership preferences. Indeed, dealing with weapon characteristics can appear to be overall an inherently hard data enterprise, simply because much (if not most) of the evaluation is bound to fall within the purview of the physical sciences. And finally there is an understandable and, in terms of current Soviet strategic arms efforts, entirely justifiable reason to concern ourselves primarily with weapon characteristics, since they are the very essence of the Soviet *capabilities* about which we worry.

We would be remiss, however, if we took any of these basic "pluses" on the side of the rational strategic actor approach as sufficient reason to avoid further investigation of the SS-6 case along multiple-approach lines or to rule out the need for future multiple-approach analyses of other Soviet strategic arms decisions. It is by no means intended to diminish the significance of focusing on capability questions to suggest that the attempt to learn all that we possibly can about how and why past Soviet strategic arms decisions were made is worth making.

Such an attempt is worth making because the Soviet strategic threat is compounded of both capabilities and intentions, however important the former. And in trying to comprehend Soviet intentions,[56] we are likely to be drawn into making social science judgments even about the significance of weapon characteristics as an indicator of these intentions.

Earlier in the study it was pointed out that one can easily fall into the trap of reading the Soviets in American and

Western terms—by, for example, hastily transplanting pluralistic decision-making notions in Soviet soil. There is a similar, and perhaps more subtle, trap to watch out for in evaluating weapon characteristics precisely because an analysis of them can rightly begin with an assumption of the universality of the behavior of physical phenomena—that is, of the same physical "laws" operating in both the United States and the Soviet Union. It is this, after all, on which a physical science evaluation of the nature of these characteristics basically depends. Yet it would be a mistake to believe as a consequence that all analysis of Soviet weapon characteristics is bound to be free of the taint of national differences and thus inherently hard. Indeed, if this analysis extends to the point where judgments are made about the significance the Soviets attach to these characteristics, such judgments are both soft and social scientific to some degree. For they involve, surely, an estimate of Soviet perceptions. These may differ from U.S. perceptions because of a peculiarly Soviet evaluation of the very nature of the weapon characteristics in question.[57] And, as the suggested relevance of Soviet command and control perspectives in the SS-6 case would indicate, these perceptions may also differ because of other uniquely Soviet considerations that are brought into play.

In the overview of the SS-6 decisions, the technical shortcomings of the first Soviet ICBM were noted and, on the basis of available information, found to be insufficient in themselves to have precluded a larger deployment of the system than the one eventually made. A detailed analysis using all available data might well reveal that in fact those shortcomings were so overwhelming that Soviet decision makers could not possibly have decided to push ahead with a sizable production and deployment effort. In that event, the significance accorded other decision-making considerations in impeding the program would then have to be diminished drastically.

In that event also, the analytic role the physical scientist might play in interpreting the weapon characteristics of the SS-6 could be such that the social scientist's role might be quite perfunctory. But this cannot be assumed at the outset of an investigation of the SS-6 decisions and certainly should not reinforce an inclination to ascribe interpretations of Soviet weapon system characteristics in other decision-making cases solely to the province of physical scientists.

All of this calls attention to the basic problem addressed in the study—namely, the assumptions analysts bring to evaluations of why Soviet strategic arms decisions occur. It is important in this regard to avoid assuming that the scope of a social science investigation of these decisions is so narrow as to preclude judgments about the significance of weapon characteristics. And it is equally important to avoid assuming that the scope of a decision-making analysis of these decisions is so narrow as to preclude consideration of such topics as weapon characteristics and strategic doctrine.[58]

As indicated in the introduction to this study, in focusing on such topics as strategic doctrine and weapon characteristics as explanations of Soviet strategic arms decisions, we make implicit assumptions about the decision making that allows these topics to "determine" decisions. Such assumptions may be valid, but then again they may not. To make some determination in this regard, these decision-making assumptions should be treated explicitly. In addition, these assumptions should be juxtaposed to contrary decision-making assumptions stressed by other interpretive points of view. And it would be no small contribution if that juxtaposition yielded only a sufficient appreciation of the strengths and weaknesses of all these decision-making assumptions to keep us properly appreciative of when we were justified in making assertions and when we were not.

As it stands, this overview of the SS-6 program, in which such a juxtaposition was made, suggests that from whatever perspective, the decision making in the case is exceedingly difficult to understand and may never be really understood. The overview also suggests, however, that we are also probably not justified in simply turning our backs on decision-making analyses and relying on such topics as strategic doctrine and weapon characteristics, which can be treated without specific reference to decision making, to carry the interpretive burden. In this regard, it would be unfair to argue that a pluralistic interpretation or a national leadership interpretation has somehow failed if it does not explain the SS-6 program as a decision-making analysis might be able to explain some U.S. weapon program. First of all, when considered in decision-making terms in the rational strategic actor approach, Soviet strategic doctrine or the weapon characteristics of the SS-6 can also probably not yield such an explanation. (In short, they are part of the decision-making "problem" as well, and not just apart from it.) More importantly, unless it is shown by subsequent analysis that a social science judgment on the significance of the performance characteristics of the SS-6 is almost perfunctory (that is, that a physical science evaluation shows that the system's shortcomings were truly overwhelming), that social science judgment should be weighed against similar judgments that can be made on pluralistic or national leadership grounds.

In that matchup, it is not legitimate to apply a double standard of evidence, which is skewed to favor one interpretive point of view and to disfavor others. One is, after all, in this case trying to estimate not only such soft and amorphous topics as interests and preferences, but another soft and amorphous topic as well: the Soviet perception of the significance of the system's technical characteristics. The point is that we should remain open to the possibility that, when all is said and done, we may have at least as much to go on in getting a fix on those interests and preferences as we do on that perception. The only way we can achieve any valid judgment on the matter is to take our analysis of each of these soft topics as far as we possibly can and to do it fairly.

A Governmental Task

Ideally, future case studies of Soviet strategic arms programs would be made as a concerted multiple-approach effort involving specialists in fields related to the programs in question. Individuals with substantial expertise in such fields as Soviet weapons, Soviet economic planning, Soviet foreign policy, Soviet political leadership, and the like would all appear to have a necessary analytic contribution to make.

The value of such an effort is underscored by considering the alternatives. Progress seems least likely to be achieved if decision-making case studies are undertaken by a single analyst hewing basically to a particular approach. Both by dint of natural talent and predisposition, a given analyst is not likely to be sensitive to a sufficiently wide variety of considerations nor capable of doing justice to those considerations that lie outside his immediate area of expertise. A single analyst utilizing multiple approaches would seem to stand a better chance of making progress. But since Renaissance men are in notoriously short supply these days, it is doubtful that one analyst's sensitivity to a variety of decision-making considerations would be coupled with the expertise needed to treat those considerations properly. There may be management problems in trying to bring a number of different specialists together to conduct multiple-approach case studies, but on the whole that seems the best way to proceed.

While the multiple approach method is very attractive in principle, it will probably be very difficult to apply. Even posing the array of questions that the individual approaches suggest should be posed in analyzing a given decision (or set of decisions) would seem to be a large task. Clearly, then, appropriate analysis to the point of arriving at an overall judgment is a tall order indeed. Similar treatment of an array of Soviet strategic arms decisions to improve our understanding of how and why those decisions are made—and the role of the action-reaction phenomenon in those decisions— would be an enormous undertaking.

Since this analysis would seem to require the use of classified materials, the role of scholars without access to these materials is likely to be limited.[59] Analysts who do not have access to classified materials can certainly help frame appropriate questions, but the main burden would appear to be on those within government with access to classified data and a professional responsibility to offer policymakers information and advice on Soviet strategic arms behavior.

It should be stressed, however, that the hopes of emulating decision-making analyses of U.S. strategic behavior would seem to be inherently limited by the probable dearth of data on the Soviet defense environment. Indeed, because of these data limitations, bona fide case studies (in the strict sense of the word) may simply not be possible. All decision-making analyses confront the problem of having to deal not only with processes but also with such soft topics as goals, interests, preferences, and the like, which are the ingredients that are processed in the making of decisions. In the Soviet case, even with the use of highly classified data in looking at a given weapon program, there is the additional problem of limited information with regard to such ingredients as well as to the process itself.

But this is precisely why multiple approaches are especially commended in analyzing Soviet strategic arms decisions. Using multiple approaches in an array of cases would also seem to be necessary. The data are likely to be too skimpy and soft to allow us to avoid decision-making approaches altogether or to put much confidence in what a single decision-making approach and a single case might tell us about how and why Soviet strategic arms decisions are made. The whole point of trying to utilize decision-making analyses in a setting in which, at first glance, they seem not to belong at all is that such analyses do compel us to confront directly assumptions we routinely make anyway and to take into account information we would otherwise overlook. Their utility in this regard would be more than undone, however, if the first halting steps to the better understanding that they make possible became but an excuse for the assertion of some new analytical dogma.

Notes

Introduction

1. Johan J. Holst, *Comparative U.S. and Soviet Deployments, Doctrines, and Arms Limitation*, Occasional Paper, Center for Policy Study (Chicago: University of Chicago Press, 1971), p. 19.

2. See Office of the Secretary of Defense, Historian, *History of the Strategic Arms Competition, US-USSR, 1945-1972* (forthcoming).

3. Colin Gray, "The Arms Race Is About Politics," *Foreign Policy*, no. 9 (Winter 1972-73), pp. 121-22.

4. This is not to imply, however, that information on technical characteristics would necessarily be all that abundant. Moreover, there can be considerable diversity with regard to interpreting the technical data, even leaving perception considerations aside. The question of the Soviet Backfire's range capability, of key importance to the strategic arms limitation talks (SALT II), is a notable case in point.

5. It would seem likely, after all, that all Soviet strategic arms decisions would not be made in exactly the same way—as a consequence of changes over time in the international context and the Soviet political context, as a consequence of differences in the technological levels of strategic arms programs, and so on. It would also seem likely that changes in decision-making processes would also affect the chances of strategic calculation, bureaucratic interests, and so forth, being brought to bear on decisions. Establishing correlations of these factors is bound to be a long and

arduous task. But it is the kind of effort that seems unavoidable, if analyses of the workings of the Soviet defense setting are to be properly responsive to the needs of the Western policymaker. He is, after all, appropriately concerned not with these workings per se, but with the kinds of decisions—the arms programs and defense policies—that result.

6. Given the tenacity of the data problem, notwithstanding the most diligent efforts, the kind of guidance one might realistically hope to acquire is in the nature of discerning broad trends and patterns rather than gaining instant revelation from the ability to penetrate to the details of a particular case. It is, of course, recognized that even without utilizing decision-making approaches, this is not an unusual way of going about the business of interpreting Soviet strategic arms programs and policies in light of the data problem. One does not ordinarily rely only on the weapon characteristics of a single system, but tries to find patterns, complementarities, and so on, by placing, say, a new Soviet system in a context of other new Soviet systems, in a context of developments in pertinent doctrine, in a context of relevant exercise practices, and so on. The argument in this study is that even with such precautions, the data net may still not get cast widely enough and too many assumptions may still go unchallenged. (Even decision-making case studies confined to but a single period in which various Soviet systems have "come on board" together would seem useful in this regard in pointing up relationships [whether complementary or competitive] in the decisions taken on those systems.)

7. In light of the previously noted point that conceptual elegance cannot make up for poor data, it may appear somewhat contradictory to argue that concepts should be called upon in a data-poor setting to serve in effect as surrogates for evidence in performing a "testing" function—that is, to be used to challenge yet other concepts where the evidence is inadequate to the task. Strictly speaking, a contradiction is involved here, but the very nature of analysis would seem to make it unavoidable, since the analyst after all has only concepts and data to work with. The alternative is to run the risk of becoming so comfortable with certain analytical assumptions that these assumptions wind up carrying an analysis largely on their own and without one's clear appreciation that they are in fact doing so. In that event, concepts really do substitute for evidence.

8. It might be noted here that underlying the social science

nature of the problem of explaining Soviet strategic arms behavior is the even more fundamental philosophical nature of the problem—which involves the relationship between the *known* and the *unknown* and how the latter affects our judgments about the former. Most rigorously treated by the great German philosopher Kant as a perennial philosophical issue, it is exemplified here in our efforts to deal with the *unknown* of how the Soviets actually decide on a given strategic arms program. We will probably never know how in even a single case. But we do *know* that this unknown matters and that we cannot therefore simply ignore it and make judgments about Soviet intentions by relying only on what we regard as known—for example, weapon characteristics. Performing decision-making analyses of Soviet strategic arms programs, despite the fact that we may not be able to carry them very far, can at least serve the useful function of helping us to better appreciate how much we do not know.

9. The taxonomy should make it apparent that there are strategic arms decisions and strategic arms decisions. No single case can be regarded as truly representative of Soviet strategic arms decision-making practices. In order to determine what practices are unique to particular circumstances and what practices are general and constant over time, classification of strategic arms decisions might proceed, *after an array of cases is in hand*, according to such broad categories as: technological level, Soviet domestic political and economic context, and international context. For example, a strategic arms program involving substantially new technologies might reveal quite different decision-making practices than one that was essentially a modification of an existing weapon system wherein off-the-shelf components could be used. Similarly, certain practices might differ according to the particular kind of weapon system, for example, aircraft versus missiles. Decision-making practices would also be likely to change to some degree according to the regime in power. They might, for example, reflect the change from Khrushchev's basic penchant for personal involvement in many policy areas to his successors' apparently greater willingness, on the whole, to leave more to the discretion of experts in various fields. (This broad difference in leadership styles is well noted in Jerry Hough, "The Soviet Succession," *Washington Post*, April 17, 1977.) And some weapon systems, judged likely to have a substantial impact on the strategic balance at a particular time, might very well be characterized by extensive top-level delibera-

tion, while others of apparently marginal importance may be treated as line-item entries calling for little real scrutiny by the top decision makers. All of these differences and more would be germane to a full-scale evaluation of Soviet strategic arms decision making and, in turn, of an assessment of the role of the international action-reaction phenomenon in Soviet decisions.

10. Graham T. Allison, *Essence of Decision: Explaining the Cuban Missile Crisis* (Boston: Little, Brown, 1971). In addition to drawing on Allison's specific approaches, this study owes his work a large and obvious debt for its basic demonstration of the feasibility and utility of applying multiple approaches.

11. By the standards of the decision-making analyses that have been applied to U.S. domestic, foreign policy, and defense decisions, the approaches used in this study are quite crude. Moreover, by the standards that have recently begun to be applied to decision-making analyses of the Soviet domestic scene, these approaches may also seem unsophisticated. Even if the approaches put forth in this study were presented for use on an individual basis, however, it would seem prudent to keep them relatively simple and strightforward. Since analysis of Soviet strategic arms decisions has not been characterized thus far by an extensive effort to confront the data in decision-making terms, it is doubtful that any decision-making approaches that might be used for this analysis can be appropriately refined at this point. Approaches can only be adequately refined—and acquire veracity—when they are made to live up to their name by actually "approaching" something. The basic task therefore is not to concentrate on refining approaches in a vacuum—which may be more misleading than helpful—but to assemble a few simple analytical tools and then try to use them.

Chapter 1

1. Graham T. Allison, *Essence of Decision: Explaining the Cuban Missile Crisis* (Boston: Little, Brown, 1971), p. 13. For a full discussion of the model, see pp. 10-66.

2. As will be discussed later, these broader political-strategic considerations can perhaps be better taken into account within the confines of a separate approach—the national leadership approach. And their relationship to strategic considerations in the strict military sense will not be lost, so long as both a rational strategic actor and national leadership approach are used together

in a multiple-approach analysis.

3. *Essence of Decision*, pp. 36-38.

4. Soviet military doctrine has by no means been neglected by Western students of the Soviet military scene—as the several excellent studies by Raymond Garthoff, Thomas Wolfe, Herbert Dinerstein, William and Harriet Scott, Matthew Gallagher, John Erickson, and others over the years will attest. Attention to this doctrine would help analysts avoid succumbing to what has come to be known as the danger of *mirror-imaging,* that is, reading the Soviets in American terms. It goes without saying, however, that in paying close attention to this doctrine we should not delude ourselves into thinking that as Western "outsiders" we can avoid bringing assumptions to it that differ from those Soviet "insiders" might hold. Try as we might, the acquisition of near native fluency in the Russian language and the most diligent study of Soviet military lore will still mean that a Marshal Ogarkov, for example, will read the very same words in Soviet doctrinal pronouncements as we do with a somewhat different understanding. And as this study as a whole seeks to show, it is in any event a continuing challenge merely to be cognizant of some of the major assumptions that we bring to our analyses of the Soviet military scene, much less to figure out how to correct for the inherent ethnocentric and other biases that our assumptions may contain when they are made explicit.

(Close students of Soviet military writings will doubtless observe that as used in this study, the term *doctrine* is a broad one—broader than the formal Soviet designation of the term. It is appropriate to note that the Soviets themselves are fussy about categorizing their military pronouncements and, given that, such distinctions as among military "art," "science," "doctrine," and so on seem useful as tools for Western analysts. For present purposes, however, it seems inappropriate to focus on these distinctions—or even to accept them at face value—in light of the larger interpretive issues at hand. For a stimulating evaluation of Admiral Gorshkov's recent writings which illustrates both the usefulness of these distinctions and the Talmudic feats they can encourage Western analysts of the Soviet scene to attempt, see James McConnell, "The Gorshkov Articles, The New Gorshkov Book, and Their Relation to Policy," in Michael MccGwire and John McDonnell, eds., *Soviet Naval Influence: Domestic and Foreign Dimensions* [New York: Praeger, 1977], pp. 565-620.)

5. The many uncertainties encountered in trying to establish a

relationship between doctrine and capabilities are incisively examined on the U.S. side of the strategic equation in Graham T. Allison and Frederick A. Morris, "Armaments and Arms Control: Exploring the Determinants of Military Weapons," *Daedalus*, 104:3 (Summer 1975), pp. 99-129. Emphasizing, in particular, time lags between the acquisition of capabilities and the formulation of doctrines, the authors underscore the difficulty of explaining the whys of a weapon program—for example, the purposes for which a weapon was developed (so far as they can be discerned) may not be the purpose(s) for which the weapon was eventually deployed, and so on. Distinctions of this sort are, for the most part, not explored in this study in order to keep the approaches and their differences as straightforward as possible. However, further refinements of these approaches should take them into account.

6. See Benjamin S. Lambeth, "The Sources of Soviet Military Doctrine," in Frank B. Horton et al., eds., *Comparative Defense Policy* (Baltimore: Johns Hopkins Press, 1974), pp. 200-16. Incidentally, it is important to bear in mind that whether the doctrine reflects "rational" purpose or "rationalization" affects basically our estimate of Soviet intentions with regard to the system in question. Obviously, from a capability standpoint, a rationalized Soviet weapon may still give Western policymakers much reason for concern.

Besides the need to be sensitive to the possibilities for professed doctrine to represent a vehicle for the rationalization of parochial service interests, there is also the need to appreciate the possibilities for professed doctrine to reflect distinctive political concerns in the USSR. In regard to the latter, it is pertinent to note that the various newspapers, journals, and books that represent the bulk of Soviet military writings are under the editorial control of the Main Political Administration (MPA), a unique institution which is both part of the Ministry of Defense and the functional equivalent of a department of the party's Central Committee Secretariat. Hence, from a circumstantial standpoint alone, even the military prose that is affected only by the blue pencils of MPA officials (since some prose originates in the MPA itself) could contain certain emphases and formulations that reflect particular political rather than military concerns and priorities. The extent to which this is likely to happen would seem to depend not only on the issue at hand but also on the basic loyalties of MPA types; that is, are they loyal to the party? to the military? to neither? to both? Much ink has been spilled over the years by Western students of the Soviet military scene trying to find the MPA's real identity—perhaps more ink than the MPA warrants when compared to other organizational entities in the Soviet defense establishment whose relevance to defense policies and weapon programs of concern to Western policymakers seems inherently much greater. For a recent excellent—and quite pertinent—discussion of the MPA's role and outlook, see Edward L. Warner III, *The Military in Contemporary Soviet Politics: An Institutional Analysis* (New York: Praeger, 1977), especially pp. 72-76. (Incidentally, in pulling together all sorts of useful information on Soviet military organizations, doctrine, and force posture, this book represents one of the best single reference works on the Soviet military. Indeed, it is perhaps more of a reference work than its subtitle really suggests.)

7. This characteristic of the Soviet decision-making environment should be appreciated, but it is easy to overstate its significance. Remarks made by the top-ranking Soviet military delegate to SALT (to the effect that the U.S. team should not reveal information on Soviet military matters to the Soviet civilian delegates) doubtless are the kinds of things that can encourage such overstatement. (Cf. John Newhouse, *Cold Dawn: The Story of SALT* [New York: Holt, Rinehart and Winston, 1973], p. 56.) But, as will be noted, there are a number of civilians in the Soviet Union who, while not strategists by profession, have a considerable body of expertise on strategic arms programs—for example, weapon designers and defense-industrialists—that the top leaders may draw on to check the views of military professionals. And of late there have also been some signs that the Soviets are trying to develop a token force of strategists, at least outside the precincts of the Ministry of Defense, if not perhaps strictly civilian (that is, in the Institute for U.S. and Canadian Studies and the Institute of World Economics and International Relations).

Chapter 2

1. Barrington Moore, *Social Origins of Dictatorship and Democracy: Lord and Peasant in the Making of the Modern World* (Boston: Beacon Press, 1966), p. 480.

2. See the discussion of Khrushchev's education reform of 1958 in Joel Schwartz and William R. Keech, "Group Influence on the Policy Process in the Soviet Union," *American Political Science Review*, 62 (September 1968). See also the discussion of policy impact on the part of interest groups in the Stalingrad Oblast in

Philip D. Stewart, *Political Power in the Soviet Union* (Indian-apolis: Bobbs-Merrill, 1968). One of the more elaborate models to be devised thus far for approaching the Soviet system in a way more consonant with broader methodological developments in the social sciences is James B. Bruce and Robert W. Clawson, "A Zonal Analysis Model for Comparative Politics: A Partial Soviet Application," *World Politics*, 24:2 (January 1977).

3. A discussion of such resistance with respect to policy implementation, as well as an assertion of lower level decison-making impact, in the repeal of Khrushchev's production education program can be found in Philip D. Stewart, "Soviet Interest Groups and the Policy Process," *World Politics*, 22:1 (October 1969).

Resistance at lower levels of the Soviet administrative hierarchy to the implementation of top-level decisions and efforts to circumvent such decisions have long been noted, in particular in the Soviet civilian economy—even in the Stalin era when the totalitarian model was accepted by most Western students of Soviet affairs. Continuity and change in regard to such resistance over the years can be discerned by reading in tandem Joseph Berliner's pioneering study, *Factory and Manager in the USSR* (Cambridge, Mass.: Harvard University Press, 1957) and his recent opus, *The Innovation Decision in Soviet Industry* (Cambridge, Mass.: The MIT Press, 1976).

4. For a survey of certain representative interest groups, see H. Gordon Skilling and Franklyn Griffiths, *Interest Groups in Soviet Politics* (Princeton: Princeton University Press, 1971).

5. The articles by Schwartz and Keech and Philip Stewart, cited above, on the decisions to inaugurate and then repeal production education in the Khrushchev era are perhaps the best examples.

6. Yet Sidney Ploss's point is well taken: "Even during the era of Stalin there was room inside the framework of Soviet dictatorship for senior bureaucratic groupings to compete for influence and to argue for policy alternatives." "New Politics in Russia," *Survey*, 19:4 (Autumn 1973), p. 35.

7. In what is perhaps the best extant critique of pluralistic analysis of the Soviet scene, William E. Odom has argued: "The most persuasive argument for the totalitarian model is to try to imagine the study of Soviet politics without it. We understand contemporary Soviet politics more by the ways in which it departs from the totalitarian model than we do through new models." From "A Dissenting View on the Group Approach to Soviet

Politics," *World Politics*, 28:4 (July 1976), p. 567. The best recent overall discussion of the need to progress beyond the totalitarian model, however, in analyzing the Soviets can be found in Jerry Hough, *The Soviet Union and Social Science Theory* (Cambridge, Mass.: Harvard University Press, 1977).

8. It is quite true, as William Odom maintains, that the concept of interest groups loses some of its distinctiveness in being applied in this fashion. But it is still open to question whether treating the Soviet government as a collection of interest groups (in the broad sense of the term) is somehow sharply distinguishable from, and woefully inferior to, analyzing the Soviet government as an arena of bureaucratic politics. As is discussed below, there are distinctions to be made between the pulling and hauling of people who head up governmental organizations (that is, bureaucratic politics, as Allison defines it) and the broad organizational interests (that is, group interests) of the particular agencies, committees, ministries, and so on, that those people head. But until we have seriously come to grips with the data to illuminate these differences as they bear on Soviet strategic arms decisions, it seems premature for present purposes to insist on a methodological purity that keeps these decision-making notions at odds and in so doing overrides the basic pluralistic bias they hold in common.

9. Graham T. Allison, *Essence of Decision: Explaining the Cuban Missile Crisis* (Boston: Little, Brown, 1971), pp. 79-80. For a full discussion, see pp. 67-144.

10. Ibid., p. 144. For a full discussion, see pp. 144-244.

11. Allison stresses the impact of constituent pressure on these players or bargainers notwithstanding other considerations that define their roles. As will be described in chapter 3, it is on this crucial point that the national leadership approach parts company with Allison's bureaucratic politics model.

12. Allison, *Essence of Decision*, pp. 113-17.

13. See, for example, Arthur Alexander, *R&D in Soviet Aviation*, R-589-PR (Santa Monica, Calif.: The RAND Corporation, 1970); *Weapons Acquisition in the Soviet Union, United States and France*, P-4989 (Santa Monica, Calif.: The RAND Corporation, 1973); and *Armor Development in the Soviet Union and the United States* (Santa Monica, Calif.: The RAND Corporation, 1976).

The role of designers, for example, would seem to be important in gauging the impact of a technological imperative in prompting

Soviet strategic arms decisions. In general, the pluralistic approach reflects the school of thought on the Soviet-U.S. arms race, described by Gray, that focuses on internal self-generating stimuli for weapon efforts (in contrast to responsiveness to adversary actions). The technological imperative implies that the urge to exploit technological possibilities is one such stimulus.

14. See Karl F. Spielmann, "Defense Industrialists in the USSR,"*Problems of Communism,* 25:5 (September-October 1976), pp. 52-69.

The evolution of the defense industrial ministries is discussed in "The Soviet Defense Industry as a Pressure Group," in M. MccGwire, K. Booth, and J. McDonnell, eds., *Soviet Naval Policy: Objectives and Constraints* (New York: Praeger Publishers, 1975), pp. 87-122.

15. Anomalies in the Soviet force posture over the years would seem to make it particularly tempting to focus on the significance of service interests in influencing certain weapons programs. David Holloway argues that one should look beyond parochial service interests, traditions, and the like to explain such anomalies. For example, he draws attention to pricing factors in the defense industries, which in the past at least may have created strong disincentives to stop the production of "obsolete" weaponry. Whether such factors should be considered more important than service pressures or not is an open question. But these factors should at least not be ignored. See David Holloway, "Technology and Political Decision in Soviet Armaments Policy," *Journal of Peace Research,* no. 4 (1974), pp. 257-79.

Chapter 3

1. Examples of this sort abound. Studies that focus on Khrushchev's concern with his ideological credentials in dealing with China in the late 1950s and early 1960s offer a particularly vivid illustration. For a comprehensive review of explicit decision-making treatments of Soviet foreign policy, see Arnold L. Horelick, A. Ross Johnson, and John D. Steinbruner, *The Study of Soviet Foreign Policy: A Review of Decision-Theory-Related Approaches,* R-1334 (Santa Monica, Calif.: The RAND Corporation, 1973).

2. This notion of national leadership decision making may be fairly close to what Allison had in mind (with respect to his models) in arguing, "But models that mix characteristics of the

three are clearly possible. One of the more interesting and promising is a cross between Model I and Model III [that is, rational actor and bureaucratic politics] . . . focusing, in the case of the United States, on the President whose purposes nevertheless include more than mere strategic values and whose activities require sneakers as well as boots." Graham T. Allison, *Essence of Decision: Explaining the Cuban Missile Crisis* (Boston: Little, Brown, 1971), p. 277.

3. Neither here nor elsewhere in the study is the term *preference* used in the sense of a mere whim on the part of a national leader. It is meant to indicate a serious personal concern, which in some way could be discerned in the leader's prior career or current behavior.

4. Weapons decisions made on the basis of strategic calculation would serve some particular organizational interests in any event.

5. See, for example, Roman Kolkowicz, *The Soviet Military and the Communist Party* (Princeton: Princeton University Press, 1967).

6. Recent forays into "psychohistory" (such as Doris Kearns, *Lyndon Johnson and the American Dream* [New York: Harper & Row, 1976]) to explain the behavior of American presidents may be fairly novel, but broadly similar efforts have been standard fare for some time for scholars of the Soviet scene trying to understand Stalin's actions. For one of the best and most recent examples, see Adam B. Ulam, *Stalin: The Man and His Era* (New York: Viking Press, 1973).

7. See, for example, Sidney Ploss, *Conflict and Decision-making in Soviet Russia: A Case Study of Agricultural Policy, 1953-1963* (Princeton: Princeton University Press, 1965).

Chapter 4

1. Raymond Garthoff, "SALT and the Soviet Military," *Problems of Communism*, 24:1 (January-February 1975), p. 29. On the council's precursors, see John McDonnell, "Control of Soviet Defense Policy," paper presented at the Ninth National Convention of the American Association for the Advancement of Slavic Studies, Washington, D.C., October 15, 1977.

2. Prior to his political demise in 1977, N. V. Podgorny was also identified as a council member. (Garthoff, "SALT and the Soviet Military.") Harriet Scott has suggested that A. P. Kirilenko and M. A. Suslov may also be members. Whether they are or not does not, however, significantly affect the basic issues under discussion here.

See Harriet Fast Scott, "The Soviet High Command," *Air Force Magazine,* March 1977, p. 53.

Differences of opinion among Western analysts regarding the membership of the Defense Council are nevertheless useful to underscore the kinds of data problems that scholars of the Soviet defense scene confront and that make the hope of ever emulating decision-making studies of U.S. weapon programs basically an idle one. These differences of opinion also extend to the lineage of the council (i.e., whether or not it is the successor to Stalin's and Khrushchev's Higher Military Council) and its exact position on Soviet organization charts (i.e., whether or not it is formally subordinated to the Council of Ministers or Politburo or neither of these bodies). In arguing that the council should not be viewed as the successor to Stalin's and Khrushchev's Higher Military Council, James McConnell has made the following vivid comparison: "To confuse these two councils . . . is like confusing our National Security Council with the Pentagon." (See "The Gorshkov Articles, the New Gorshkov Book, and their Relation to Policy," in Michael MccGwire and John McDonnell, eds., *Soviet Naval Influence: Domestic and Foreign Dimensions* [New York: Praeger, 1977], p. 614.) What matters for present purposes is not whether McConnell is correct on this point but that his remark calls attention to the enormous gulf that separates analyses of Western and Soviet defense decisions. It is a sobering reminder that the kind of information that would obviously be regarded as very basic common knowledge for scholars assessing a U.S. weapon program can be still an object of some uncertainty and debate for those looking at Soviet programs.

3. It might be noted that acknowledging the possible relevance of other than strategic concerns, when decisions have to be made on strategic arms programs, does not necessarily run contrary to the argument that top decision makers might be inclined to "simplify" inherent complexities in these strategic concerns per se in order to make decisions on them manageable. That argument is effectively advanced in John Steinbruner, "Beyond Rational Deterrence: The Struggle for New Conceptions," *World Politics,* 28:2 (January 1976), esp. p. 236.

4. It also cannot be excluded that these Politburo members might have personal contacts with individuals in the defense sector—contacts that would permit them to secure, "independently," information necessary for knowledgeable criticism of decisions emerging from the precincts of the Defense Council.

They might, for example, have personal contacts with key military personnel or one or more of the principal supervisors of the defense sector (besides D. F. Ustinov, L. V. Smirnov, chairman of the Military-Industrial Commission, and I. D. Serbin, head of the Defense Industry department of the Central Committee have recently served as supervisors for the top leadership); ministers and possibly deputy ministers of the defense industrial minisitries; and key weapon designers. For a discussion of the possibility of such contacts, see Karl F. Spielmann, "Defense Industrialists in the USSR," *Problems of Communism*, 25:5 (September-October 1976), especially pp. 62 and 64.

Malcolm Mackintosh has provided an intriguing example of civil-military contacts at another level, which is also useful in helping us to keep a balanced perspective on the nature and extent of compartmentalization in the Soviet defense setting. He notes that at a Central Committee Plenum in June 1967, N. G. Yergorychev, first secretary of the Moscow City Party Committee, appears to have criticized recent Soviet policy in the Middle East war and to have been demoted as a consequence. Mackintosh suggests that, in his capacity as a member of the military councils of the Moscow Military District and Moscow Air Defense District, Yegorychev may have been "put up to" the role of critic by military types uneasy about the state of Soviet air defenses at the time of the Middle East war, and, as a consequence, uneasy about the possible escalation of the war because of Soviet policies. For present purposes what is significant about all this is that if Mackintosh is correct at least about Yegorychev's contacts with the military, it behooves us to be cautious about assuming that even more highly placed officials (that is, Politburo members) would be routinely kept in the dark about important military matters. See Malcolm Mackintosh, "The Soviet Military: Influence on Foreign Policy," *Problems of Communism*, 22:5 (September-October 1973), pp. 6-7.

5. This consideration is admittedly not easy to appreciate if one thinks of the Soviet economy as being simply a war-mobilization economy. High priority for defense, however, hardly means that the Soviets regard other economic purposes as trivial. Moreover, as will be discussed below, broader foreign policy concerns should be included under the civilian rubric. These concerns could skew defense programs away from what military professionals might advise on strategic grounds even while detracting from certain domestic economic programs.

6. Five-year plans have been standard for the Soviets since the

late twenties, with the notable exception in the postwar period of a seven-year plan that ran from 1959 through 1965. Given the lead-time problem, defense planning may also include plans of a longer duration. Coordination with the overall economic plan is, however, likely to make the annual and midterm defense plans particularly important. The existence of these plans is noted in A. Baranenkov, "Financial Support to the Troops Under Annual Planning Conditions," *Rear Services and Supply of the Armed Forces*, no. 10 (1972), pp. 57-61; and V. Dutov, "Improving Economic Operations in the Army and Navy," *Communist of the Armed Forces*, no. 2 (January 1972), p. 34.

7. One should be cautious, in any event, in assuming that Soviet five-year defense plans would be as detailed and as set in concrete as the popular image of the Soviet overall economic plan would suggest defense plans might be. Gregory Grossman has argued that these overall economic plans for the five-year period may have been much more amorphous than the Soviets have let on. "In the postwar period, these plans have customarily been reported by quite brief and ostensibly tentative documents, such as the present 'Basic Directions' [that is, for the 1976-1980 plan] . . . and only in the case of the Ninth FYP [that is, for 1971-1975] . . . were they followed by the publication of a more or less comprehensive, book-length document. There is some reason to believe that in most or all cases before 1972 no final version was published simply because no agreed-upon comprehensive plan was completed, although this fact was never publicly admitted." Gregory Grossman, "The Brezhnev Era: An Economy at Middle Age," *Problems of Communism*, 25:2 (March-April 1976), p. 25.

It also might be noted that even if defense plans are reasonably detailed and comprehensive, certain priority weapon system programs may simply be permitted more flexibility than others in terms of abiding by plan criteria. Ballistic missiles have been cited in this regard in David Holloway, "Soviet Military R & D: Managing the Research-Production Cycle," in John R. Thomas, ed., *Soviet Science and Technology*, published for the National Science Foundation by the George Washington University (Washington, D.C., 1977), p. 199, and Michael Agursky, *The Research Institute of Machine-Building Technology*, The Hebrew University of Jerusalem, The Soviet and East European Research Centre, Soviet Institutions Paper no. 8 (September 1976), pp. 33-34.

8. See David Holloway, "Technology and Political Decision in Soviet Armaments Policy," *Journal of Peace Research*,

no. 4 (1974), p. 260.

9. Allison, for example, assumes that this oligarchic political situation well reflects the assumptions of his bureaucratic politics model. He does not, however, take note of such phenomena as the role of the Defense Council and defense planning which, as postulated, probably diminish the scope and frequency of top-level bargaining in defense decisions. And he assumes the importance of constituent pressure on individual top leaders, which (if one takes a national leadership perspective into account) would by no means fully explain the impact of pluralistic elements on defense decisions. See Graham T. Allison, *Essence of Decision: Explaining the Cuban Missile Crisis* (Boston: Little, Brown, 1971), pp. 182-83.

Chapter 5

1. For a classic study in this vein, which stresses the primacy of power considerations over genuine policy concerns in Soviet power struggles, see Roger Pethybridge, *A Key to Soviet Politics: The Crisis of the Anti-Party Group* (New York: Praeger Publishers, 1962).

2. Allison's bureaucratic politics model, for example, does not pay appropriate heed to these differences. He asserts that "the dominant feature of bureaucratic politics in the Soviet Union is the continuous 'struggle for power.'" Graham T. Allison, *Essence of Decision: Explaining the Cuban Missile Crisis* (Boston: Little, Brown, 1971), p. 182.

For a contrary view on the nature and extent of conflict among the ruling elite in the USSR, which stresses the Soviet leaders' appreciation of the need to abide by certain "rules of the game" to hold power struggles in check, see Thomas W. Wolfe, *The Military Dimension in the Making of Soviet Foreign and Defense Policy*, P-6024 (Santa Monica, Calif.: The RAND Corporation, 1977), pp. 31-32; Dennis Ross, *Rethinking Soviet Strategic Policy: Inputs and Implications* (Los Angeles, Calif.: Center for Arms Control and International Security, 1977), p. 21; and Dimitri K. Simes, *Detente and Conflict: Soviet Foreign Policy 1972-1977* (London: SAGE, 1977), p. 49.

3. On Soviet organization charts, the VPK would occupy a formal position above governmental ministries, including the Ministry of Defense.

4. See Raymond Garthoff, "SALT and the Soviet Military,"

Problems of Communism, 24:1 (January-February 1975). It should be noted that from the regime's perspective the VPK would be viewed not merely as a forum in which pressure from below could be exerted on the regime, but as a mechanism to exert top-level control. Depending on the decision, it probably could serve either purpose.

5. The services are Strategic Rocket Forces, Ground Forces, National Aerospace Defense Forces, Air Forces, and Navy. The current defense-industrial ministries are Defense Industry, General Machinebuilding, Medium Machinebuilding, Radio Industry, Electronics Industry, Machinebuilding, Aviation Industry, and Shipbuilding. (It is possible that a ninth ministry has existed since April 1974—the Ministry of Communications Equipment Production. The evidence to this effect is, however, quite skimpy.) For a discussion of these ministries and their weapon responsibilities, see Karl F. Spielmann, "Defense Industrialists in the USSR," *Problems of Communism*, 25:5 (September-October 1976), p. 54.

6. It is unclear at present whether Ustinov's appointment as minister of defense on April 29, 1976, has in fact deprived him of a continuing role in overseeing defense production efforts. Ustinov's life-long involvement in administering weapon programs suggests that, in some fashion, his supervisory interest and activity may persist. However, he no longer is listed as a Central Committee secretary and a new secretary, Ya. P. Ryabov (formerly head of the Sverdlovsk Oblast party committee), has been named and may have taken Ustinov's old job. Ryabov's address to the Soviet defense "society" (DOSAAF) congress in January 1977, for example, suggests he has some defense responsibility. See Foreign Broadcast Information Service, *Soviet Union*, February 1, 1977, p. vi.

7. See, for example, Harvey M. Sapolsky, *The Polaris System Development: Bureaucratic and Programmatic Success in Government* (Cambridge, Mass.: Harvard University Press, 1972).

8. This image is, of course, not confined to the defense sector. It is part and parcel of widely held assumptions about the special qualities and capabilities that members of the Communist Party possess and that make it possible for the Soviet leaders to maintain the upper hand in controlling a vast and complex society. This view is epitomized in the following statement: "The distinguishing characteristic of a party member is that he can be counted on to subvert the sub-unit's self-interest." (See William E. Odom, "A Dissenting View on the Group Approach to Soviet Politics,"

World Politics, 28:4 [July 1976], p. 554.) The Soviets, to be sure, may be closer to achieving this subversion among party members who are only party functionaries in contrast to party members who are also scientists, economic managers, professional soldiers, and so on. But even among the functionaries, the image of a "new Soviet man" should not be blithely accepted. No doubt the leadership has aspired to create party members who are immune to selfish interests and entirely devoted to serving the national interests of the Soviet state as a whole (as the leaders supposedly define them). But it is surely giving the Soviets too much credit to assume that, in this case as in others, what they aspire to they automatically achieve.

9. See, for example, A. S. Yakovlev, *Tsel' Zhizni: Zapiski Aviakonstruktora* [The target of life: notes of an aircraft designer], trans., FTD-HT-23-956-67 (U.S. Air Force Foreign Technology Division, Wright-Patterson Air Force Base, Ohio, 1967), especially p. 395.

10. Note that in such cases the national leadership approach would have a contribution to make in explaining the decision in any event. While one could never be sure exactly where leadership preference left off and lower level impact began, the emphasis on the preferences of the top leaders in the national leadership approach calls attention to a factor that must be taken into account in making even a rough judgment one way or the other. Otherwise, in weapon system decisions regarding which the lobbying efforts of, say, a designer were in evidence, one would be inclined simply to assume successful pressure or influence.

11. Note that while a defense-industrial ministry would not be likely to snub an important service customer, these ministries have a bargaining leverage that would seem to be generally greater than defense producers in the United States. The National Aerospace Defense Forces (PVO Strany) has no alternative but to deal with the Ministry of the Aviation Industry to secure a desired interceptor. The Strategic Rocket Forces has similarly no alternative but to deal with the Ministry of General Machinebuilding for certain major categories of missile systems, and so on.

12. This might come about for a variety of reasons: the minister may have a personal antipathy toward the designer; the minister may view the program as a particular burden from a management standpoint (for example, involving unwanted dependencies on other ministries); or the minister may see the program as challenging the continued production of certain "old" systems

that may yield the ministry a better economic return. The first point is at least hinted at in Yakovlev, *Tsel' Zhizni*, p. 398. On the second point, see Spielmann, "Defense Industrialists in the USSR;" on the last point, see David Holloway, "Technology and Political Decision in Soviet Armaments Policy," *Journal of Peace Research*, no. 4 (1974).

Chapter 6

1. Colin Gray, *The Soviet-American Arms Race* (Westmead, Eng.: D.C. Heath, 1976), p. 30.

2. *Report of Secretary of Defense James R. Schlesinger to the Congress on the FY 1976 and Transition Budgets, FY 1977 Authorization Request and FY 1976-1980 Defense Programs*, February 5, 1975 (Washington, D.C.: Government Printing Office), p. II-2. Incidentally, one should bear in mind that in certain major respects Soviet "capabilities" are not solely in the hands of the Soviets to determine. For example, the hard-target kill capability of a Soviet ICBM is a matter of the characteristics of potential targets as well as the characteristics of the missile.

3. See Benjamin S. Lambeth, "The Evolving Soviet Strategic Threat," *Current History*, 69:409 (October 1975).

4. *Report of Secretary of Defense James R. Schlesinger*, February 5, 1975.

5. Some might argue, however, that prompting the Soviets to consider options planning would not necessarily be a bad thing. Should the Soviets, for example, launch limited strikes ad hoc fashion in a crisis situation, their lack of planning for further limited follow-on strikes could leave them no alternative to a limited U.S. response but "capitulation" or escalation to all-out nuclear war.

6. Throughout this discussion the action-reaction phenomenon is considered in terms of Soviet reaction to U.S. action. This expression of the phenomenon is presumably of most interest to U.S. policymakers concerned with the whys and wherefores of Soviet defense decisions, since it is important to know whether and to what extent the decisions they make could affect Soviet behavior. Those concerned with the motives behind U.S. behavior would be equally interested in U.S. reaction to Soviet action. And finally, one might note that another expression of the action-reaction phenomenon that should be legitimately considered is in the relations between the Soviet Union and its other major strategic

rival, the People's Republic of China.

7. Herbert York, "ABM, MIRV, and the Arms Race," *Science,* July 17, 1970, p. 257. For an expansion of these views, see also *Race to Oblivion* (New York: Simon and Schuster, 1970).

8. These technical organizations have been specifically identified in at least the Ground Forces and the Air Forces. See John Milsom, *Russian Tanks, 1900-1970* (Harrisburg, Pa.: Stackpole, 1971), p. 80; and Raymond Garthoff, "Soviet Air Power: Organization and Staff Work" in Asher Lee, ed., *The Soviet Air and Rocket Forces* (New York: Praeger Publishers, 1959), p. 181.

9. See Arthur Alexander, *Weapons Acquisition in the Soviet Union, the United States, and France,* P-4989 (Santa Monica, Calif.: The RAND Corporation, 1973), esp. pp. 8-11. Memoir material has focused attention on the roles played by designers in the defense scientific establishment. However, the attitudes and potential clout of research scientists also should be considered. These scientists may, for example, be less wary than the designers about technological dynamism, given the latter's direct responsibility to turn out practicable weapon systems.

10. See Karl F. Spielmann, "Defense Industrialists in the USSR," *Problems of Communism,* 25:5 (September-October 1976), esp. pp. 59-61.

11. Note also, at another level, the growing prominence in recent years of the Institute for U.S. and Canadian Studies (IUSAC) and especially its director, George Arbatov. Insofar as the initiation of SALT may have prompted such developments, SALT per se should be heavily scrutinized in terms of its potential effects on Soviet decision-making practices—for example, perhaps in generally "politicizing" strategic arms decisions and in specifically making certain action-reaction "linkages" more manifest to the Soviets than they otherwise would have been. On the SALT experience in general, see: Center for Strategic and International Studies, Georgetown University, *Soviet Decision-making, Strategic Policy and SALT,* ACDA/PAB-243 (Washington, D.C.: U.S. Arms Control and Disarmament Agency, December 1974); and *Soviet Strategic Policy and Decision-Making,* R-1686 (Santa Monica, Calif: The RAND Corp., September 1975).

12. See Raymond Garthoff, "SALT and the Soviet Military," *Problems of Communism,* 24:1 (January-February 1975), p. 29.

13. It would be going too far, however, to suggest that strategic arms decisions would be shaped by broader politico-strategic concerns heedless of basic military considerations. And, of course,

to the extent that such concerns worked to enhance the image of Soviet power in the eyes of potential adversaries, they themselves could well serve a military purpose of first priority—namely, deterrence. A general Soviet attentiveness to image considerations in military policies and a narrower U.S. focus on combat effectiveness is well argued in a recent study. See Edward N. Luttwak, *The Missing Dimension of U.S. Defense Policy: Force, Perceptions and Power* (Alexandria, Va.: Essex Corporation, February 1976). This contrast, by the way, would seem germane to an evaluation of the extent to which it makes much sense to sharply juxtapose a U.S. emphasis on deterrence to a Soviet stress on war-fighting.

And this contrast also raises intriguing questions about the significance of a related comparison often made of the U.S. and Soviet defense establishments—namely, that in the nuclear age civilians have shaped American strategic thinking while the professional military have done so in the Soviet case. In gross terms at least, one would think that this should mean that the Soviet setting would be more conducive to an emphasis on narrow military considerations and the U.S. setting more amenable to broader foreign policy concerns in devising military policies. This is not the place to deal with such apparent anomalies or contradictions, but it should be noted that they merit investigation, and the general point emphasized that even if the hoariest generalizations about American and Soviet strategic behavior are basically correct, they may nevertheless really explain very little.

14. See especially Colin Gray, "The Arms Race Is About Politics," *Foreign Policy*, no. 9 (Winter 1972-73), pp. 117-29.

15. Such concern would seem to underlie, for example, former Secretary of Defense James Schlesinger's testimony on the implications of a Soviet limited nuclear options capability for U.S. relations with its North Atlantic Treaty Organization (NATO) partners. See Secretary of Defense James R. Schlesinger, Testimony before U.S. Congress, Senate Foreign Relations Committee, Subcommittee on Arms Control, International Law and Organization, 93rd Cong., 2d sess., March-April 1974, esp. p. 197.

16. It might be noted, however, that when the promotional effort reaches the top of the line, broader politico-strategic considerations may well be stressed by military spokesmen to ensure better (or wider) receptivity by the top political leaders. Admiral Gorshkov's recent writings on the Soviet Navy are a good example of this attentiveness to political or broader foreign

policy concerns. See Admiral Gorshkov, *Red Star Rising at Sea*, Theodore A. Neely, Jr., trans. (U.S. Naval Institute, 1974) and *The Sea Power of the State* (Moscow, 1976).

17. In narrowing the rational actor model to focus specifically on strategic calculation in the military sense, the role of broader politico-strategic values is, of course, deliberately circumscribed in the rational strategic actor approach. As has been argued earlier in setting out the rational strategic actor approach, this focus is intended to facilitate efforts to gauge the strategic weight of Soviet strategic arms programs. On the basis of the discussion presented above, it should also be apparent that there is another benefit that accrues from a separation of strategic values into military and nonmilitary categories: namely, it avoids the assumption that the same decision-making rationale would necessarily underpin the impact of both.

Chapter 7

1. After all, it was not until 1974 that an effort got under way in the U.S. government to provide a comprehensive history of Soviet and U.S. strategic arms programs and policies in the postwar era. See Office of the Secretary of Defense, Historian, *History of the Strategic Arms Competition, US-USSR, 1945-1972* (forthcoming). This study promises to be at the very least an important point of departure for any future historical treatments of Soviet strategic arms efforts. And it would be an unfortunate irony—quite contrary to the spirit in which the authors undertook the study—if the very existence of the study was used to justify continued inattention to the past by other analysts as pressing policy needs were being met.

2. Analyses of such controversial programs as the Backfire bomber, for example, might particularly benefit from the use of a frame of reference that takes into account what the situation of the relevant service element(s) was when the program got under way. Would the Long Range Air Force [LRA] (a branch of the Air Forces), in this case, have been most concerned at the time about its future theater mission or intercontinental role? For which purpose would it have been most easy for the LRA to secure the backing of other service components at the time? (The Backfire is also deployed with Naval Aviation.) Could the LRA have realistically hoped to secure the go-ahead for two separate (that is, heavy and medium bomber) programs simultaneously? Could the

LRA have tried to hedge the bets by pushing a program that could potentially serve both theater and intercontinental purposes? Since the Soviets currently have a new heavy bomber under development (see Helmut Sonnenfeldt, "Russia, America and Detente," *Foreign Affairs,* [January 1978], p. 278)—which is presumably intended to enter the inventory of the LRA—what does that program suggest for LRA perspectives on the Backfire? Would original LRA views on the potential significance of the Backfire for an intercontinental strike role have changed subsequent to the authorization of this new heavy bomber program? Would that program have been authorized in the first place if the Backfire had been intended for such a strike role? These are but samples of the kind of questions that a historical perspective on the Backfire might yield and that might contribute to current efforts to assess the program.

3. Since there has been no dearth of efforts to interpret the arms race between the U.S. and USSR (or even to chart defense spending trends), such efforts may also tend to obscure the fact that, by and large, a systematic investigation of the evolution of Soviet strategic arms programs has, until very recently, not been made. A somewhat more egregious misperception of the extent to which the *relevant* past has been taken into account could stem from the fact that, over the years, a veritable smorgasbord of pat characterizations of the Russian historical experience in general has been assembled, which analysts can select from to give their interpretations of particular Soviet strategic arms efforts the appearance of being grounded in solid historical investigation. Such notions as the "traditional" Russian search for warm-water ports, the "traditional" Russian fear and dislike of the Chinese yellow peril, the "traditional" Russian defensive mentality, and the like may on occasion have some analytical utility. But these notions, in the first place, are not beyond dispute—and hence should not be merely trotted out as axioms of Russian-Soviet behavior—and, in the second place, stand a good chance of being less relevant to an interpretation of some Soviet strategic arms program than the more near-term historical data which they can entice one to neglect. Even if one were to approach these notions in a more serious fashion, therefore, that would still amount to a skewing of analytical priorities. At a time when we have barely begun to dig earnestly into the history of Soviet strategic arms programs in the postwar era, it would be an indulgence to encourage the kinds of studies that could wind up

favoring us with such perversities as an analysis of, say, the significance of the political machinations of medieval Russia to Soviet negotiating behavior—perhaps though wittily entitled "The Belskiis, Shuiskiis, and SALT: The Boyars and the Bomb."

4. Without splitting methodological hairs, it is pertinent to note the distinction between two kinds of unknowns: the *unknown* whose very existence we do not (and cannot be expected to) know and the *unknown* that we know exists at least to the extent that we can acknowledge it as a potential factor in a particular context. The former can, of course, wind up ultimately affecting the *correctness* of our conclusions. But that unknown cannot affect (logically) the *validity* of the argument that led to those conclusions and in which it was, by definition, excluded at the time the argument was put forth. How the Soviets actually decide on a given strategic arms program is not, however, this kind of unknown.

5. Another kind of omission that specialization might tend to encourage is in basic estimates of Soviet concerns to attain (or consolidate?) strategic nuclear superiority over the United States. It is, of course, appropriate that questions of the technical feasibility of such a course of action and its basic implications for whether the USSR would "push the button" should get priority treatment. Yet in focusing on them, deliberate consideration of another seemingly quite relevant factor can get short shrift— namely, to what extent would the Soviets be prone to view the possession of strategic nuclear superiority as conferring real foreign policy assets in peacetime (that is, without strategic nuclear weapons actually being used or their use deliberately threatened in conflict situations)? This factor could affect the accuracy both of an estimate of Soviet concerns to attain (or consolidate?) strategic nuclear superiority and an estimate of the basic implications of such superiority. It is surprising, in light of the crucial issues at stake here, how sparse the serious treatment of this factor has been in the recent literature, when compared to the attention given to such matters as the technical feasibility of Soviet strategic superiority and whether the Soviets view a nuclear war as winnable. (Besides the Luttwak study cited in chapter 6, the following can be especially recommended as valuable aids in efforts to come to grips with this problem: Ken Booth, *The Military Instrument in Soviet Foreign Policy, 1917-1972* [R.U.S.I., Whitehall, London, 1973]; Hannes Adomeit, *Soviet Risk-Taking and Crisis Behavior*, Adelphi Paper no. 10 [London,

1973]; R.J. Vincent, *Military Power and Political Influence: The Soviet Union and Western Europe*, Adelphi Paper no. 119 [London, 1975]; and Robert Legvold, "The Nature of Soviet Power," *Foreign Affairs*, 56:1 [October 1977].)

6. Analogy to the Western experience with Nazism would seem to provide a powerful reinforcement to the urge to give Soviet ideological pronouncements perhaps more than their due. After all, the mistake made in ignoring Hitler's blueprint in *Mein Kampf*—the argument might run—should not be repeated in the case of the Soviets.

7. Much of what has been said in this discussion applies as well to our treatment of that special part of the ideology contained in Soviet military writings. In that case, for example, we must guard against slipping into a kind of circular reasoning in which: (1) the observable characteristics of some weapon are first interpreted on the basis of certain assumptions we may hold about the Soviet strategic outlook; (2) our perusal of Soviet military writings is then guided by what the weapon's characteristics tell us; and (3) lo and behold, we find passages in these writings that support our interpretation. We might then proceed to the final step of arguing that the congruity of weapon characteristics and doctrine observed in this instance demonstrates the reliability of the doctrine as a guide to Soviet strategic behavior.

8. If one were to be consistent in adhering to the notion that quotes count and increase the roster of legitimate analytical contestants, there is a good chance that quite often the regime's quotation collectors could win hands down. Incidentally, denying that Soviet behavior in a particular case is ideologically motivated (and is, for example, guided rather by a hard-headed "nonideological" notion of Soviet national interest) by pointing to the absence, or even scarcity, of appropriate remarks in the articulated Soviet ideology also reflects an implicit acceptance of the special methodological role of Soviet ideological pronouncements—an acceptance that likewise begs many questions.

9. This is not to slight the many efforts that have been made over the years to refine our approaches to the Soviet ideology (and incidentally our approaches to the concept of ideology per se, as well, as exemplified in the writings of Karl Mannheim, George Lichtheim, and others). Useful distinctions have been drawn which differentiate "chiliastic" goals, the Soviet "action program," the subtle shaping influence of certain inchoate Marxist categories on the thought processes of the Soviet leaders, the

instrumental role of the ideology as a legitimizing factor in the Soviet polity, and so on. But while such distinctions themselves help to illustrate the complexities involved in trying to utilize Soviet ideological pronouncements for guidance, they can also create the mistaken impression that all we really need to get the problem well in hand is an approach that is sufficiently sophisticated. (Similar observations apply to our ability to differentiate such concepts as military art, military science, military strategy, and military doctrine in looking at Soviet military pronouncements. These concepts, as developed by the Soviets themselves, are useful aids to interpretation, but they can help delude us as well into thinking that we are much closer than we really are to a firm understanding of the relationship between military pronouncements and Soviet strategic programs and policies.)

10. Sound scholarship would require not only establishing what those ultimate goals might be but also that they would in some fashion (to be at minimum regarded as meaningful) shape even relatively long-range planning on the part of the Soviets. From the standpoint of relevance to present concerns, this, of course, still begs such huge questions as: the relationship between long-range plans and short-range plans (so far as Soviet priorities are concerned); the projected tractability of events to Soviet ambitions (there is, for example, in this regard always the danger of practicing a kind of strategic Lysenkoism in viewing the Soviet plans—that is, to assume that the Soviets have a magic formula for bending the world to their wishes); the willingness or unwillingness of the Soviets to alter their plans accordingly; and so on—a daunting analytical menu to say the least.

11. This is not to deny that very solid research may have been done (and may be doable) on all sorts of things about Russian peasants, both today and in centuries past. Nor is it to deny that out of such diligent investigation some generalizations about behavior traits of Russian peasants might be distilled. But that, of course, would be only the starting point for any reasonably sound effort to explain the perspectives of current Soviet leaders on strategic arms matters in light of Russian peasant experience. How does one tell if that experience would outweigh quite different attitudes garnered by a leader, say, from his training as an engineer? How does one tell if current social status or job responsibilities or a host of other factors that go to make up one's attitudes matter more? Obviously there is reason to suspect an

analysis that would give answers to such questions without first even explicitly asking them. In reaching into the past (especially a past that may be neither relatively immediate nor part of a leader's personal experience), there is a special obligation on the part of the analyst to demonstrate not only the soundness of his analysis of the past experience he wishes to draw upon but also the relevance of that experience. Otherwise, if blithe assertion is to carry the day, one might, in fastening onto the peasant past to explain Soviet perspectives on strategic arms, for example, expect common sense to favor an argument that cited not the Russian peasant's approach to violence and coercion but rather his simple preoccupation with things agricultural as his primary and enduring trait! And what would one make of that?

12. To be sure, what makes our understanding more than just guesswork is that, for example, some research can be (and has been) done on such factors as age, education, occupation and so on in elite analyses of Soviet officials. That this is unlikely to lead to much more than informed guesswork, however, so far as giving us real guidance to the policy predilections of a new leader, is suggested by considering (mirror-image fallacies notwithstanding) how effectively we could chart the course of American politics if we could look at no more than we can in the Soviet case. This, by the way, is a useful mental exercise to perform in looking at, say, one of the great windfalls for sovietologists in recent years: Khrushchev's memoirs. Establishing the authenticity of the memoirs, as important as that is, only just begins to tackle the problem. Since we are well aware that different officials in the United States frequently give us quite different interpretations as insiders of the very same events, it behooves us to bear constantly in mind that, lacking a similar basis for comparison, we are still quite handicapped in looking to Khrushchev's memoirs (however authentic) as a reliable source.

13. It should be apparent from the discussion that in not attaining the sophistication needed to really meet the needs of policymakers, the aforementioned model could also not in any strict sense purport to be *the* (or even the best) model of Soviet civil-military relations. Presumably that qualification would be met when one was in a position to detemine whether the model really worked in at least more cases than it did not.

14. Exceptional cases might not be easy to recognize even when the data provide strong hints to an analyst of a conceptual ill-fit. But a rich data base in a particular case would at least seem to

increase the chances that a conceptual ill-fit would be exposed—
and that is a luxury the Soviet setting does not readily make
available to us.

15. Without venturing too far down what are essentially
epistemological byways, it is worth noting that the failure of the
model to predict accurately what it purported to predict would
also tend to indicate the exceptional nature of the case at hand.
However, this is far from foolproof self-correction, since the
model that failed in making the prediction would, of course, also
produce an inherently biased explanation of the failure.

Chapter 8

1. For example, how representative is the program of U.S.
estimates of the size of the Soviet threat over the years?
(Cf. Albert Wohlstetter, "Racing Forward? Or Ambling Back?"
Survey, 22:34 [Summer-Autumn 1976], pp. 169-170.) It is hardly
consistent with the premises of this study to offer any present
judgment on this score. Those concerned with what the program
suggests about the nature of the estimative process in the United
States and U.S. arms race behavior can also usefully consult:
Edgar M. Bottome, *The Missile Gap: A Study of the Formulation
of Military and Political Policy* (Cranbury, N.J.: Fairleigh
Dickinson University Press, 1971); Roy E. Licklider, "The Missile
Gap Controversy," *Political Science Quarterly,* 74:4 (December
1970); Colin S. Gray, " 'Gap' Prediction and America's Defense:
Arms Race Behavior in the Eisenhower Years," *Orbis,* 16 (Spring
1972); and James C. Dick, "The Strategic Arms Race, 1957-61:
Who Opened a Missile Gap?" *Journal of Politics,* 34:4 (November
1972).

2. Arnold Horelick and Myron Rush, *Strategic Power and
Soviet Foreign Policy* (Chicago: University of Chicago Press,
1965), p. 83.

3. Cf. ibid., p. 83 *passim.*

4. "The possibility that the Soviet Union might be engaged in
a crash program to build and deploy a large force of first generation ICBMs was not rejected by the United States government
until early 1960. Intelligence estimates of the Soviet ICBM
program were reduced accordingly, but they still projected a far
larger Soviet force for 1961 than was actually credited to the USSR
in that year." Ibid., p. 36.

5. Nikita S. Khrushchev, *Khrushchev Remembers: The Last*

Testament (Boston: Little, Brown, 1974), p. 52.

6. Horelick and Rush put this consideration into the broader context of Soviet estimates regarding U.S. intentions at the time. Drawing attention to other weapon systems the Soviets pushed ahead with, notwithstanding technical problems, they argue that the Soviets might well have gone forward with the SS-6 if the risks of war with the United States had been appreciable in the late 1950s and early 1960s. They argue that the Soviets believed that risk to be very low; hence they were prepared to wait for a better system. *(Strategic Power and Soviet Foreign Policy,* pp. 106-8.) This line of reasoning would have required the Soviets to display admirable sang-froid for a country having to live with a large intercontinental bomber gap at the time in the U.S. favor. (By 1960, for example, the United States had roughly a 3:1 advantage in intercontinental bombers.) This would, however, hardly have been the first time that the Soviets had to live with a U.S. edge in strategic arms (the U.S. postwar nuclear monopoly being a particular case in point). But it may well be asked, Did the international climate change so drastically in the early 1960s to warrant a precipitate abandonment of this Soviet patience? Emplacing missiles in Cuba displayed a much greater degree of Soviet impatience than seems explicable in terms consistent with the Horelick and Rush line of reasoning. For a country that had been "conditioned" to live with a U.S. strategic edge, surely an increase in international tensions in the early sixties (which the Soviets precipitated to a considerable degree; for example, Berlin in August 1961) and an awareness of the growing missile gap in favor of the United States should have led to no more than a big push in the Soviet ICBM effort at that time. If one counters by arguing that Khrushchev wanted to catch up with the United States "on the cheap" by the Cuban ploy then attention is drawn to the salience of Soviet nonstrategic priorities in the early 1960s. But surely these priorities were not all that less salient in the late 1950s, when a determined push in the SS-6 program was foregone. In short, Soviet patience in the late 1950s may have been one factor—and indeed an important factor—in inducing the Soviets to wait on a better missile system, but its significance should not be overstated.

7. *Khrushchev Remembers,* p. 50.

8. William H. Schauer, *The Politics of Space* (New York: Holmes and Meier, 1976), p. 13.

9. Other shortcomings as well were pointed out by Khrushchev

in his memoirs, such as that the system had guidance problems and was "vulnerable" because it was soft-launched (*Khrushchev Remembers*, p. 48). In order to evaluate how formidable the Soviets actually regarded these shortcomings in the late 1950s, one would have to ask such questions as the following. Did the Soviets avoid those shortcomings in the successor system(s) to the SS-6? And if so, how quickly? In other words, was the successor system that much better than the SS-6 in respect to both accuracy and hard-launch capability that it made sense to avoid a sizable deployment of the SS-6 as even a stopgap? Accuracy problems would presumably have detracted considerably from the use of the SS-6 as a counterforce weapon, but in the Soviet perspective, would they seriously have undermined the countervalue role of the SS-6—for example, as a deterrent? Finally, could Khrushchev's emphasis on the shortcomings of the SS-6 in his memoirs be attributed to a need on his part to come up with a posthoc rationalization for the failure to deploy the SS-6 in large numbers—a decision that he (and other Soviet leaders) took on quite other grounds at the time and for which he was subsequently criticized? (It is only fair to note yet another shortcoming that Western analysts have emphasized, namely the sheer size and weight of the SS-6 [see, e.g., George H. Quester, *Nuclear Diplomacy* (New York: Dunellen, 1970), p. 193].) The system apparently was huge even by Soviet standards and this doubtless would have posed special problems for its military use. Yet before assuming that for the Soviets this would have made the SS-6 seem *prohibitively* awkward, it is useful to remember that (1) the system was extensively used in the Soviet space program; and (2) even after the Soviets later reached a level of warhead technology where more of a premium could be placed on designing rockets that were easier to handle, other values presumably intruded to make it attractive for the Soviets to turn out, say, the large SS-9 and its successor, the SS-18.

10. Johan J. Holst, *Comparative U.S. and Soviet Deployments, Doctrines, and Arms Limitation*, Occasional Paper, Center of Policy Study (Chicago: University of Chicago, 1971), p. 24.

11. The apparent technical shortcomings in the SS-6 program are useful in pointing up the relationship between physical scientists and social scientists in evaluating Soviet strategic arms decisions. Clearly, physical scientists are needed to evaluate available data on technical characteristics. As suggested with regard to Soviet command and control perspectives, however, what

the technical characteristics might mean to the Soviets may be quite different from what they might mean in the United States. That evaluation would seem to call for a social science contribution.

12. Horelick and Rush, *Strategic Power and Soviet Foreign Policy*, p. 31. There had been, however, some preliminary tests in spring 1957 (see Dick, p. 1070).

13. See Leon M. Herman, "The Seven-Year Haul," *Problems of Communism*, 8 (1959), p. 9.

14. It cannot be ruled out that production and deployment decisions were in fact taken earlier and were stuck to subsequently. But the nature of the program and the setting in which it came to fruition strongly suggest that these decisions were either postponed as long as possible or that changes were made in the original decisions, or both.

15. The Soviet reaction would not necessarily have been to U.S. missile efforts. The reaction element in the SS-6 program at this stage might more plausibly have been to the growing bomber gap in the U. S. favor. On the other hand, a reaction to the apparent Western intent in late 1957 to push IRBMs in Europe (which was itself a reaction to the appearance of the SS-6) could have affected Soviet interest in beefing up their own M/IRBM effort and, ironically, indirectly redounded to the detriment of the SS-6 program. (On the Western reaction, see Thomas W. Wolfe, *Soviet Power and Europe, 1945-1970* [Baltimore: Johns Hopkins Press, 1970], p. 141f.) Incidentally, this sort of Soviet reaction could have been taken as simply a rational strategic actor decision. But to the extent that the Western IRBM effort strengthened the hand of Soviet M/IRBM proponents (and to the extent that their lobbying in a period of plan preparation could shape defense priorities more than if they sought to do so when a plan was under way), pluralistic decision making could also have reflected this reaction element. All of this gives but a hint of the kinds of complexities one can encounter in trying to determine the role of the action-reaction phenomenon.

16. How the activities of groups pushing parochial interests may contribute to decisions that seem eminently rational is a complex topic that has only been touched upon in this paper. The topic ultimately merits the detailed attention that such theorists as Robert Dahl and Charles Lindblom have paid to the positive role of multiple interest inputs into U.S. domestic decisions. For the present, it is sufficient to emphasize that a

decision on, say, the production and deployment of a particular weapon system may turn out to make good sense (in rational strategic actor terms) as a consequence of competing pressures that, for example, compel the advocate of the system to curb his aspirations. Parochial interests could also make a contribution to a decision by alerting top decision makers to ramifications of a weapon system that might otherwise not have occurred to them. The decision that results may therefore be a rational strategic actor decision, in the sense of being determined basically by the strategic calculation of the top decision makers, but it would be a product of parochial interests as well. The effect of the latter would be in the nature of advice (or, if you will, influence) but not, strictly speaking, pressure. It would not be surprising if many Soviet strategic arms decisions were of this sort, since at bottom they would seem to well reflect a decision-making context in which the top leaders have considerable power but lack omniscience.

17. The pulling and hauling is basically suggested by two considerations. First, even if one picks August 1957 (when the successful SS-6 test was held) as the earliest date that the Soviets became aware that they had to think seriously about the service jurisdiction of ICBMs, it still took a long time to sort out the question. Since it took more than two years (from this point) to establish a new service arm to accommodate the ICBM, service resistance to such a course of action seems likely. Second, after the SRF was set up, the Soviets (and, apparently, particularly Khrushchev) accorded it a primacy that was bound to disgruntle the traditional services. By the latters' reckoning, the emphasis given the SRF not only violated the sacred combined arms tradition of the Soviet military establishment, in principle, but also apparently led to some shifting of resources to their detriment—for example, the manpower cuts that ensued in 1960, following Khrushchev's "New Look" speech to the Supreme Soviet in January of that year. If the established services had any inkling in the late 1950s that the establishment of an SRF would have such implications, their resistance to it could hardly have been surprising.

18. Graham T. Allison, *Essence of Decision: Explaining the Cuban Missile Crisis* (Boston: Little, Brown, 1971), pp. 114-15.

19. An analysis of even the service interest in MRBMs should address the question of whether the overall service

interest would have been strong, or whether only the branch within the service specifically charged with MRBM responsibility would have had a strong interest. As earlier pointed out, one should not automatically assume an intensity of interest in a weapon system at the service level that might only accurately reflect the point of view of part of that service. It is well to remember that MRBMs were also relatively new weapons, and they might not have been all that attractive to more traditional military types, even within the particular service that had formal jurisdiction over them.

20. *Khrushchev Remembers*, p. 50.

21. Ibid., p. 51.

22. See, for example, Arthur Alexander, *Weapons Acquisition in the Soviet Union, the United States, and France*, P-4989 (Santa Monica, Calif.: The RAND Corporation, 1974), p.10.

23. Leonid Vladimirov, *The Russian Space Bluff* (New York: Dial Press, 1971), p. 47.

24. Schauer, *The Politics of Space.*

25. Alexander, for example, notes that the bulk of weapon design resources in the Soviet Union are held by the defense-industrial ministries. See *Weapons Acquisition.*

26. See, for example, Andrew Sheren, "Structure and Organization of Defense-Related Industries," in U.S., Congress, Joint Economic Committee, *Economic Performance and the Military Burden in the Soviet Union* (Washington, D.C.: Government Printing Office, 1970). Interesting insights into the workings of this ministry and the Ministry of Machinebuilding are also offered in Michael Agursky, *The Research Institute of Machinebuilding Technology: A Part of the Soviet Military-Industrial Complex*, Soviet Institutions Paper no. 8 (Soviet and East European Research Centre, Hebrew University of Jerusalem, September 1976).

27. *Khrushchev Remembers*, p. 51.

28. For a rundown of this ministry's responsibilities, see Sheren, "Structure and Organization."

29. Robert A. Kilmarx, *A History of Soviet Air Power* (New York: Praeger Publishers, 1962), p. 253.

30. Thomas W. Wolfe, *Soviet Power and Europe, 1945-1970* (Baltimore: Johns Hopkins Press, 1970), pp. 179-80ff.

31. Cf. the speech by A.F. Zasyadko reprinted in *Izvestiya*, May 10, 1957, p. 4.

32. The exception was the Ministry of Medium Machine-building, the custodian of Soviet nuclear production efforts for the military.

33. For a discussion of the jurisdictional question with regard to research and development and production as it pertained to the economic reorganization as a whole, see Alexander G. Korol, *Soviet Research and Development* (Cambridge, Mass.: The MIT Press, 1965), pp. 16-18.

That the ministries lost some responsibilities is also suggested by the transfer of certain key defense-industrial administrators to central administrative posts (most notably, D.F. Ustinov, current defense minister, long-time defense sector overseer and, prior to December 1957, minister of the Defense Industry Ministry). The need for beefing up central direction of the defense effort at the time would have been strong, if it became necessary to coordinate the defense production effort carried out under the regional economic councils and smooth the basic research and development and production relationship between the state committees and these councils. For an excellent discussion of the job transfers of key officials and their implications, see John McDonnell, "The Soviet Defense Industry as a Pressure Group," in M. MccGwire, K. Booth, and J. McDonnell, eds., *Soviet Naval Policy: Objectives and Constraints* (New York: Praeger Publishers, 1975), pp. 98-101.

34. Michel Tatu, *Power in the Kremlin* (New York: Viking Press, 1969).

35. The word *presumably* should be stressed. We cannot automatically assume that earlier career affiliations continued to shape their views. This speaks to a general problem one confronts in trying to identify the likely policy preferences of Soviet leaders. Do earlier career ties to particular individuals or organizations really matter? Do current job slots really permit firm identification of policy preferences? William Odom has argued that even the latter question cannot be answered with certainty—and that it may be useful to consider the possibility that, as party members, Soviet personalities may act contrary to what their particular organizational affiliation might indicate. Until such possibilities have been investigated in depth, however, it seems more reasonable to assume that, say, a minister of agriculture would be "'interested' in getting more machinery for agriculture" than that he would not. See William E. Odom, "A Dissenting View on the Group Approach to Soviet Politics," *World Politics*, 28:4 (July

1976), p. 554.

36. Tatu, *Power in the Kremlin,* p. 137. See also, on Kozlov's defense interests, William Hyland and Richard Shryock, *The Fall of Khrushchev* (New York: Funk and Wagnalls, 1968), esp. p. 76. A useful brief overview of Kozlov's career can be found in Carl A. Linden, *Khrushchev and the Soviet Leadership, 1957-1964* (Baltimore: Johns Hopkins Press, 1966), pp. 236-237.

37. Institute for the Study of the USSR, *Prominent Personalities in the USSR* (Metuchen, N.J.: Scarecrow Press, 1968), p. 7.

38. Although we have confined the possible role of interest-group pressures in the SS-6 decisions to the defense bailiwick, a pluralistic approach could logically extend to a consideration of civilian interest groups as well. And strictly speaking, such an analysis should be done to determine where pluralistic pressure might have begun and personal leadership preference left off in shaping possible impingements on the SS-6 program. An analysis of pluralistic pressure, by the way, should of course not be limited to an examination of lower level organizational interests in the defense establishment in any event but to the extent possible should reflect, as well, top-level political "bargaining." This was not done in laying out the pluralistic perspective in order to make as vivid as possible the difference in emphasis between that perspective and the national leadership approach. Some analysts might well contend that even in the 1957-59 period of concern here Khrushchev was more affected by pluralistic pressures brought to bear by various rivals and opponents in the top leadership circles that he was moved by personal concerns and preferences as a national leader. For present purposes all that can be ventured by way of arguing that the pluralistic approach should not be conceded greater plausibility on its face is that: (a) as indicated in the text there are some important policies and programs in the 1957-59 period linked to Khrushchev that can be explained on national leadership grounds; and (b) in this period Khrushchev seems on the whole to have been more in charge than he was either earlier or later. For an interpretation of Soviet behavior in the Berlin crises of 1958-59 and 1961, which is based on the assumption that a continuing struggle for power took place in the Khrushchev period and that Khrushchev was subjected "at all times" to internal pressures affecting both Soviet domestic and foreign policies, see Robert M. Slusser, "The Berlin Crises of 1958-1959 and 1961," in Barry Blechman and Stephen S. Kaplan, *The Use of the Armed Forces as a Political Instrument*

(Washington, D.C.: The Brookings Institution, 1976) and *The Berlin Crisis of 1961: Soviet-American Relations and the Struggle for Power in the Kremlin, June-November 1961* (Baltimore: Johns Hopkins University Press, 1973).

39. William Shelton, *Soviet Space Exploration: The First Decade* (New York: Washington Square Press, 1968), pp. 280-283.

40. Vladimirov, *The Russian Space Bluff*, p. 57.

41. Ibid., p. 75.

42. And this suggests the operation of an action-reaction phenomenon affecting the SS-6 program that one might easily overlook.

43. *Khrushchev Remembers*, p. 47.

These brief remarks by Khrushchev on Soviet space efforts do not, of course, suffice to make a case that Khrushchev's particular politico-strategic concerns clearly skewed decisions on the SS-6 ICBM effort. They do, however, suggest that it is by no means unrealistic to suppose that Soviet political types could bend strategic arms programs to serve broader foreign policy purposes even in instances where those purposes might override strictly military considerations voiced by military planners and strategists. It is not that the politicos would willfully ignore expert military opinion (which would represent a fairly unrealistic postulation of a national leader's outlook), but that they would simply place that opinion in a broader context of concerns and priorities while convincing themselves that they were not jeopardizing the country's security in doing so.

To speculate briefly in this regard with respect to Khrushchev's space program concerns, let us consider the following. As noted earlier (see note 13, chapter 6), it has been argued by some that the Soviets have been particularly attentive to image considerations in designing their force structures over the years. As also noted, that attentiveness does not have to run afoul of, for example, efforts to meet combat effectiveness criteria as well, but it would nevertheless seem to have the potential to do so on occasion. Furthermore, although military personnel may for various reasons be appreciative of image considerations (even when these conflict somewhat with combat effectiveness requirements), Soviet political types would seem, on the whole, to be particularly sensitive to them because of the broader foreign policy utility of these considerations. Especially given the performance drawbacks of the SS-6, it may well have been generally appreciated by both Soviet political and military types that even a sizable deployment of the first generation ICBM would in any event mainly serve the purpose of deterrence (which is, after all a militarily important "image" consideration). It may have been further appreciated, however, at least by Khrushchev, that Soviet space successes—as very visible indicators of Soviet missile progress and prowess— could in their own way to some extent act as a surrogate for actual deployments, serving the purpose of deterrence while also having a broader foreign policy utility. Notwithstanding other Soviet capabilities at the time (MRBMS, bombers, and so forth), Soviet military planners, for their part, would have had reason to be concerned that if put to the test it was certainly riskier to have in effect no ICBM capability at all rather than a merely questionable one. Hence, while Khrushchev may have convinced himself that space efforts were not really impinging on Soviet military requirements, there may have been more than a few skeptics in the Ministry of Defense.

44. Joseph W. Willett, "The Recent Record in Agricultural Production," in U.S. , Congress, Joint Economic Comittee, Hearings, *Dimensions of Soviet Economic Power,* 87th Cong., 2d sess., December 10 and 11, 1962, p. 107.

45. Ibid.

46. Sidney Ploss, *Conflict and Decisionmaking in Soviet Russia: A Case Study of Agricultural Policy, 1953-1963* (Princeton: Princeton University Press, 1965), p. 123.

47. Tatu, *Power in the Kremlin,* p. 32.

48. One analyst has emphasized that the Soviets suspended testing of the SS-6 from April 1958 to March 1959 and suggests that "work on it ceased until a more advanced model could be devised." (Dick, "The Strategic Arms Race," pp. 1069-70.) The rough coincidence of the beginning of the test suspension and the March MTS decree may, of course, only be that—a coincidence. It is entirely possible that, for example, the Soviets were anyhow only planning to hold a test, say, in May or June after the (implied) test in March, hence making it possible that the suspension decision actually came much later than the absence of a test in the interim would indicate. Nevertheless, it is also possible that the decision to suspend testing was taken in the same context as the decision to issue the MTS decree. Since even that is speculative, it would be even more speculative to suggest what the possible trade-offs involving the SS-6 program and agricultural mechanization might have been. On the face of it, *both* would appear to have had to yield to

other priorities in the spring of 1958.

49. Ibid., p. 168.

50. Ibid., p. 169.

51. Ibid.

52. Sheren, "Structure and Organization," p. 128.

53. Whether this concern was purely a personal preference or was at least in part a response to interest-group pressure by Soviet agricultural types is, however, difficult to say without appropriate analysis. In any event, the personal preference factor seems, in the context, quite significant.

54. Another concern of the Soviets—and doubtless of Khrushchev personally—that would appear to merit careful scrutiny in evaluating the SS-6 program is the China factor. While it is difficult to know whether or not the Chinese were apprised of Soviet production and deployment plans with regard to the SS-6, their behavior would suggest they were not and hence, like many in the West, fell prey to Khrushchev's exaggerations. Since the Chinese, in the late 1950s, sought to press the Soviets to pursue the foreign policy interests of the bloc more boldly, with this new weapon in hand, Khrushchev's boasts may well have helped to bring on the Sino-Soviet split. Soviet reluctance to be bolder (by the lights of the Chinese) would then have probably seemed to the Chinese as basically a reluctance to help out the USSR's major ally. How an anticipation of such consequences of a policy of minimal SS-6 deployment combined with braggadocio may have affected Soviet deliberations on the SS-6 program is hard to say. If the Soviets (and especially Khrushchev) surmised that this policy would tempt the Chinese to put the USSR to the test, this consideration would seem to have argued for a sizable SS-6 deployment. As Horelick and Rush have maintained, a key premise of the Soviet view at the time was that the USSR could afford to wait on a better weapon system because the risks of war with the United States were low (see note 6, chapter 8). In the fall of 1958 (that is, during the seven-year plan preparation period), the Chinese apparently sought to test both Soviet and Western resolve by commencing the Quemoy-Matsu crisis. It seems likely that this would have shaken Soviet confidence in their ability to avoid the risks of war and accordingly have then prompted some second thoughts about the prudence of minimal deployment of the SS-6. (Incidentally, beginning on November 27, 1958, the Soviets commenced a bold move of their own by issuing an ultimatum to the West with respect to Berlin. Perhaps the desire

to convince the Chinese of Soviet boldness helped precipitate this move. But at least in pushing on Berlin the Soviets could hope to keep a determination of the level of tension in their own hands— and not in those of their erstwhile major ally.)

55. It would also be premature to argue on behalf of the representative nature of the SS-6 case, except as illustrating that even on an unclassified basis we can make some headway in utilizing multiple approaches to probe Soviet strategic arms decisions. It is recognized that to some extent the SS-6 case may be special because of the availability of special source material, such as Khrushchev's memoirs. And it clearly is a special case insofar as it deals with a relatively small but not insignificant category of Soviet strategic weapon systems—that is, systems that the Soviets basically refrained from deploying. It also should be stressed that, strictly speaking, the jury should remain out on the SS-6 case until determined efforts have been made to conduct decision-making case studies of other weapon systems and defense policies in the same time frame that could have competed with or complemented decisions on the SS-6. Those that come readily to mind, such as the aforementioned Soviet MRBM or the successor ICBM, may be only the most visible candidates, but there were doubtless others (both strategic and nonstrategic) that shaped Soviet deliberations on the priority to assign to the SS-6 program.

56. The SS-6 case points up how questions of intention and questions of capability can be interrelated in complex ways. In the late 1950s, the intention question that was particularly vexatious was the extent and nature of likely Soviet production and deployment of the SS-6 so that one would know what Soviet ICBM capabilities the United States would have to deal with in the early 1960s. Of particular concern was whether the Soviets intended to field a sizable force of SS-6s. Underlying that question was the even more worrisome one (and ultimately the most worrisome question that any threat evaluation confronts) of what the Soviets intended to do once they had those capabilities in hand. But addressing these basic questions of intent involved, among other things, examining the system's capabilities, so far as its performance characteristics could be discerned and evaluated, before the extent of the deployment was in fact known. In short, certain capabilities discernible in the late 1950s were germane to an assessment of the Soviet intent to achieve certain other capabilities in the 1960s, which in turn were germane to an assessment of Soviet intent to threaten the United

States in the early 1960s.

57. National difference can matter even when our analysis of Soviet weapons characteristics is confined to relatively straightforward technical evaluation. It is one thing to broadly acknowledge that Soviet and U.S. design philosophies, scientific styles, and the like might differ. It is quite another for a U.S. physical science analyst to be appropriately aware of the subtle ways such factors might affect his evaluation, even when he tries to make allowance for them. In general, it is useful to bear in mind that although the physical scientist has an edge on the social scientist with respect to the control (and hence verification) possibilities permitted by his subject matter, "doing science" also has its share of hunch, chance, and implicit assumption. For a vivid illustration, see, in this regard, James D. Watson, *The Double Helix* (New York: Atheneum, 1968). For a systematic analysis that points up the paradigmatic nature of inquiry in the physical sciences and hence challenges the very notion of scientific "objectivity," see Thomas Kuhn's classic, *The Structure of Scientific Revolutions* (Chicago: Chicago University Press, 1970), 2d ed. (Incidentally, Kuhn's analysis, in focusing on the notion that different conceptual frameworks [paradigms] have set the standards for what is regarded as scientifically objective in different historical periods, implicitly raises provocative questions about the existence and effect of distinctively *national* paradigms [for example, U.S. and Soviet] even in the current era of extensive scientific internationalism. Perhaps the danger of mirror-imaging, which many have fastened on as *the* interpretive bete noire in viewing the Soviets, is a bit more pervasive than we have tended to suspect. Perhaps it even skews the analyses of those who go out of their way to assure that the uniqueness of the Soviet strategic outlook is fully appreciated.)

58. We can more easily overlook weapon characteristics and strategy as topics that should be considered (and indeed featured) in decision-making terms outside the purview of interpretations such as the pluralistic and national leadership approaches, which are more in line with what we usually regard as decision-making analyses. Clearly to some extent these characteristics (for example, that the system in question is an ICBM and not an MRBM or bomber) would be looked at in evaluating organizational interests or leadership preferences. And strategic doctrine could of course be viewed as an indicator of, for example, service interests, as many analysts would contend it should be.

59. The difficulty of dealing with Soviet strategic arms decisions on an unclassified basis is, by the way, apparent in the lack of any substantial decision-making case study in the open literature. Small forays into this field have been made from time to time, such as in Graham Allison's treatment of the Soviet side in his Cuban missile crisis study. And, of course, there is no dearth of generalized pieces on the Soviet-U.S. arms race. But to the author's knowledge, no decision-making case studies have appeared (and none can be expected to) that have any resemblance whatsoever to such studies on U.S. weapons decisions as Harvey M. Sapolsky's *The Polaris System Development: Bureaucratic and Programmatic Success in Government* (Cambridge, Mass.: Harvard University Press, 1972) or Michael Armacost's *The Politics of Weapons Innovation: The Thor-Jupiter Controversy* (New York: Columbia University Press, 1969) or Ted Greenwood's *Making the MIRV: A Study of Defense Decision-Making* (Cambridge, Mass.: Ballinger Publishers, 1975) or Edmund Beard's *Developing the ICBM: A Study in Bureaucratic Politics* (New York: Columbia University Press, 1976).